Joel & Naomi Mitchell
THE MARRIAGE INVESTORS

shattered

HOW TO OVERCOME A
BROKEN MARRIAGE

"This book provides a biblically sound blueprint
for husbands and wives to move from hurt to whole
by using God's word. Read it now!"

—LAMAR & RONNIE TYLER, Founders, Black & Married With Kids,
Ebony Magazine Power 100 List

All Scripture quotations, unless otherwise indicated, are taken from the King James Version, Public Domain. Scripture quotations marked "ESV" are taken from The Holy Bible, English Standard Version. Copyright © 2000; 2001 by Crossway Bibles, a division of Good News Publishers. Used by permission. All rights reserved. Scripture quotations, marked "NIV" are taken from the Holy Bible, New International Version®. NIV®. Copyright © 1973, 1978, 1984 by International Bible Society. Used by permission of Zondervan. All rights reserved. Scripture quotations marked "NKJV" are taken from the New King James Version®.

Printed in the United States of America.

Shattered:
How to Overcome a Broken Marriage

Joel and Naomi Mitchell
contact@TheMarriageInvestors.com

Copyright © 2019
ISBN 9781985199491

Published by Joel and Naomi Mitchell
www.TheMarriageInvestors.com

Dedication

To the inspiration for this book:

Our three beautiful, intelligent and gifted children
Jasper, Jacobi, and Sidni.

Thank you all for your love, patience,
and hours of sacrifice as we worked to complete this book.

One of our greatest prayers is to leave you an example and a
legacy of love and enlightenment that will bless you, your future
spouses, your children, and generations to come . . .

We love you all dearly.
May the Lord continue to order your steps. *Psalm 37:23*

Mommy and Daddy

Shattered

Acknowledgments

We give thanks and praise to God for blessing us and giving us this gift of marriage and allowing us to be the first partakers and ambassadors for Christ in the ministry of reconciliation.

Special thanks to Mom and Pops for showing us that a marriage can last a life time. Congratulations on your 51st wedding anniversary!

Special thanks to Momma Hazel for your selfless sacrifice of love, loyalty, and devotion. May you continue to rest in the love of Jesus Christ our Lord and Savior!

Thank you to our brothers and sisters — Val and Larry, Olice, Don, Mike (in memoriam), Erskine and Melanie, Robby and Belinda, Jenice, Helen, and Deborah for all of your love and support throughout our lives. To our nieces and nephews, thank you for filling us with joy and laughter!

Thank you to our covenant brother and sister, David and Kelly Moses, who the Lord placed in our lives to be our partners through this marriage and parenting process.

Thank you to Rev. Dr. Oscar T. Moses, Dr. Jacqueline Moses, and Mount Hermon MBC, the place where we met, fell in love, and were joined in holy matrimony fifteen years ago.

Shattered

Thank you to Rev. Dr. James Dunn, Sis. Jan Dunn, and the Saint John Church Baptist family for nurturing our ministerial gifts.

Thank you to our pastor, Rev. Dr. Alan V. Ragland, Dr. Barbara Ragland, and the Third Baptist Church for welcoming us with open arms and encouraging us to move forward in ministry.

Thank you to Pastor William R. and Sister Criss Lott, who mentored and nurtured Naomi to become the godly wife she is today. We love you both!

Thank you to our Board of Directors for The Family and Marriage Institute of Chicago for your love, support, prayers, and helping to undergird the vision: Rev. T. Tyrone and Quincella Roberson, Pastor Christopher and Dr. Adrienne Armstrong, and Deacon William and Vicki Mitchell.

Thank you to our writing coach, Tara Pringle Jefferson, for helping us bring our vision to pass. You are amazingly gifted!

Thank you to our publisher, Marilyn N. Alexander and PublishAffordably.com, for pulling it all together.

To Julian B. Kiganda and JBK Brand Design, thank you for the amazing cover and excellent counsel.

Thank you to Ronnie and Lamar Tyler for your selfless gift of giving, leading, mentoring, training, challenging, correcting, and encouraging!

Thank you to our web designer, Marsha "Olivia" DuCille of Called Design, who took our vision and ran with it!

Thank you to the countless married couples who have entrusted us to walk with them on their journeys of love and marriage.

Table of Contents

Shattered

Introduction

As we write this, we are only days away from our fifteenth anniversary. As anyone who has been married for more than a minute can tell you, it's been quite a ride.

Our marriage definitely didn't start out bumpy. When we tell you that our wedding was a picture-perfect day, believe it. Everything about our wedding day was designed to bring God glory.

We were married on Good Friday, and picked the colors red (to symbolize the blood of Jesus) and white. We also had communion together in remembrance of Christ's awesome sacrifice that afforded us the opportunity to come together in holy matrimony.

We had a wedding party of over thirty people — groomsmen, bridesmaids, junior bridesmaids, junior groomsmen, praise dancers, you name it. (All these years later, people are still upset that they couldn't stand up in our wedding!) We also had 500 people in attendance at the ceremony and 400 people at the reception!

The whole day was a celebration, and it really was our community rallying around us to make sure that our marriage got off to the best start possible. This was our witness for Jesus. We knew that we had been called together for a purpose, and we were serious and excited to fulfill this call with the one person in the world we loved most, next to God. Some people remarked that our wedding was more like a production than a wedding. Though some of them may have meant it sarcastically, we really were intentional about telling our story through the songs, poetry, Scriptures, and dance. Everything was planned in remembrance of Christ's love and sacrifice that was and is an integral part of our story, the Psalm of Joel and Naomi.

So later on, when we found ourselves at a crossroads in our marriage, we were first stunned and then disillusioned. We thought, perhaps naïvely, that when the enemy tried to creep into *our* marriage, we would be more prepared, especially since we'd committed our lives and our marriage to God. But we were still ambushed — not because our marriage was not blessed or we were incompatible, but because we were human. And for human people in a human marriage, trials and hard times will surely come.

We know that the people picking up this book may be in the midst of one of those trials. Your marriage may be experiencing brokenness. There has been some event — infidelity, loss of trust, unmet expectations, illness of a spouse or a child, deferred dreams, loss of a loved one, unemployment, unexpected care of an aging parent, blended family issues, you name it — that has shattered your confidence in your marriage, and you're not sure what to do next. You're wondering, *Is there something faulty in my marriage?*

We all want a solid marriage, a partnership with someone who stands beside us as our equal. But when something happens to rock that boat, how do you remain upright? How do you stay strong in your commitment?

For many couples, once they get to the dark storms, it's easy to think, *I made a mistake*. We start looking through the history of our relationship, digging to find red flags that we must have missed, things we should have done differently. We wonder if we should have dated longer or asked more questions. We wonder, *Did anyone else see the signs that trouble was ahead, and if so, how did we miss it?* Those storms shake our confidence in our vows and in the commitment we pledged before God.

But a rocky marriage doesn't have to mean a dead marriage.

The pain of a rocky marriage is a throbbing, unrelenting pain. And as humans, we're wired to make that pain go away, through our fight-or-flight response system. Do we stay and fight the stressor, or do we run from it? In some situations, you may feel like doing both, which leads to more confusion.

Let's say your first instinct is to run. Run away from your spouse and possibly into the arms of another. The pain may be so great that you think, *I'd be happier with someone else. It's time to start over.* It's easy to imagine that the problem isn't the situation itself, but the other person in the relationship. You think to yourself, *I won't have these problems in the next relationship.*

From what we've seen, those problems *will* travel with you to the next relationship if you don't do the work—first on yourself and then on your relationship. The underlying issues in a shattered marriage are usually long-simmering. You have to bring them out into the light and dissect them. Only then can you persevere.

The beauty in this pain is that God has given us a plan. He has given us the solution to marital discord throughout the Holy Bible, and particularly here, in 2 Corinthians 5:16-21:

> *So from now on we regard no one from a worldly point of view. Though we once regarded Christ in this way, we do so no longer. Therefore, if anyone is in Christ, the new creation has come: The old has gone, the new is here! All this is from God, who reconciled us to himself through Christ and gave us the ministry of*

reconciliation: that God was reconciling the world to himself in Christ, not counting people's sins against them. And he has committed to us the message of reconciliation. We are therefore Christ's ambassadors, as though God were making his appeal through us. We implore you on Christ's behalf: Be reconciled to God. God made him who had no sin to be sin for us, so that in him we might become the righteousness of God. (NIV)

God tells us where to begin — by being reconciled to Him. We cover the beginning of the reconciliation process in chapter 2, but briefly, we can tell you that you have to start at the source — with God. At its core, the ministry of reconciliation is about forgiveness, but there are steps you have to take before you are ready to forgive. Skip a step and you make the process much harder for yourself. (Unnecessarily, we might add.)

How We Can Help

We are a husband-and-wife team who have dedicated our life to helping marriages flourish, both through our work as the founders of the Family and Marriage Institute of Chicago and as relationship experts at TheMarriageInvestors.com.

We launched our institute in 2013, because as pastoral counselors, we noticed a disturbing trend: people just weren't equipped to have strong, durable marriages. There was so much focus on the engagement and the wedding and practically none on the marriage itself. People were going into this institution blind, fumbling around for advice to help them grow as a couple. But as divorce has become more and more common, even among Christian couples, there are fewer examples of what it looks like to persevere through the hard times.

There is also a stigma around going to counseling in general, and marriage counseling specifically. But we've seen firsthand how counseling can help deal with seemingly small issues before they create big problems. When a rock hits your windshield and leaves a crack, you can usually get it repaired without replacing the whole thing — as long as you act while the crack is small. If you continue to drive around and ignore it, you risk something else hitting it and making it larger, or shattering it completely. Then you've got a really costly repair bill on your hands.

That's where we were. If both of us hadn't peeled back the layers and truly committed to doing the work, we might not still be married today. Something else could have come along and shattered the great thing we were trying to build.

But we reached out for help. We prayed, both individually and together. We turned toward each other. We reached outside the marriage for guidance. We sat with a counselor and discovered new things about each other.

In short, we found our way forward, together.

Now, it is the privilege of our lives to be able to facilitate that same process for other couples. We consult couples who come to our offices and travel around the country delivering our message of reconciliation at marriage retreats and workshops. There are few things more satisfying for us than to help strengthen a marriage and help each person within it thrive.

Can We Make It like It Was?

The two of us have seen many shattered couples come through our doors. They all have one major thing in common: they're hurting. If you are in the thick of it, we know you'd give anything to feel whole and put together, but you're unsure if you can ever get to that place again.

We're not promising that if you read this book, you'll get the relationship you had in the beginning. There is no rewind button, no matter how much you wish one existed. Instead, we're promising that what's in front of you will be better than what is behind you. When people go through these challenges, they say, "I want it how it used to be." But after you've had a breakdown, you probably won't ever go back to how it used to be. What you can do is to go forward and have something new.

This truth brings to mind the ancient Japanese art of *Kintsukuroi* (also called *Kintsugi*), which means "golden repair." In this art form, broken pottery pieces are given new life after they are repaired with a golden lacquer. Google a few pieces of this art, and you'll quickly see that the true beauty is in the cracks, which are now filled with gold. With this philosophy, what was once a flaw is now what makes it beautiful.

This is what our marriage reconciliation process is designed to do. God helps you to take the broken pieces of your marriage—and make it beautiful.

Contrary to some of the messages you may hear from family and friends, you don't have to throw it away! You can have a brand-new relationship with the same pieces. It's not about forgetting what has happened, but taking the lesson and applying it to your future. God gives us the opportunity to choose love, to choose to fight for our marriages.

We have to reframe how we see the pain. Of course it's going to change what our marriage looks like. Pain changes everything. We're never the same after things have happened to us. Joel likes to joke that he can look at his high school pictures and know that he probably won't ever get down to that weight again. But that doesn't mean that he can't appreciate the body he has now.

And truthfully, if we keep it all-the-way real, you probably don't even *want* your old relationship back. If it was perfect before, then how did the brokenness occur? There were probably old wounds simmering under the surface before it erupted.

No, in truth, you want something *better* than you had before. And the good news is that it's possible. God can give you a whole new marriage.

WIll tHe paIn Go away?

We know you've picked up this book because you may be hurting. Perhaps, you're trying to figure out how to put the pieces of your marriage back together. We're good at telling people what they should do. But they need to know how. The how is missing. They can read the principles all day but when it comes down to it, *how* do you do it?

In this book, we'll be sharing composite stories from couples we've consulted over the years. All names and identifying characteristics have been changed. But we think it's important for you to understand that the issues we are discussing are real-life problems many couples face. It doesn't mean that you can't overcome them.

And let us make this very clear in case you were wondering: we don't believe every troubled marriage *should* be saved. In cases of physical, mental, emotional and/or sexual abuse, our advice is always the same — get yourself to a safe place. We know that one of the most dangerous times for a victim of domestic abuse is in the days and weeks after they leave an abusive partner. So plan your exit carefully and make sure you take care of your mental and emotional wellbeing. "Happy ever after" is for the individual to define. In cases like these, it may very well mean learning how to move on peacefully.

As pastoral counselors, we take a comprehensive and faith-based approach to healing. We believe that through Christ, all things are possible. Marriages can be rebuilt, brokenness can be mended, and hope can be restored.

However, we also know that faith without works is dead. We have to put action behind our prayers and give God something to work with. Marriages are under attack from every direction, and the more tools you have in your arsenal, the better. This book is our labor of love, a gift to you as you work on your marriage, because in most cases, with the right tools, we believe that marriages won't just survive — they will thrive.

Chapter One

Broken Glass

Evelyn sat on the couch and smoothed out the wrinkles in her skirt. She glanced at her watch. Marcus was ten minutes late to their therapy session. It was unlike him to be late, but these days, Evelyn felt she was often in the dark with what was really going on with her husband.

This was their third visit to a marriage counselor since Evelyn discovered two months earlier that Marcus had been having an affair. She knew they had drifted apart in recent years, but she never thought he would violate his marriage vows. To say she had been stunned was an understatement.

Marcus and Evelyn had met on the campus of the University of Chicago, where she was finishing her pre-law degree and he was in business school. They got married shortly after she graduated, and last summer had celebrated their tenth wedding anniversary. It had been a good ten years, although they had gone through rough patches like every other couple. Lately, the demands of parenting their three kids, ages eight, seven, and five, had caused them to think less about each other and more about their kids' basketball practice, school projects, and endless loads of laundry.

Still, Evelyn had been convinced they were just going through another rough patch. So what if they didn't have that much time with each other? She wasn't completely happy, but she was committed. She thought her husband felt the same.

The night she found out about the affair, Evelyn had been cleaning the kitchen, scrubbing the countertops and humming softly to herself while she got out the stains from that night's dinner. The kids were playing video games in the living room, laughing and joking with each other. In that moment, Evelyn felt completely at peace.

Marcus came home late from work that evening. When she saw his face, she immediately knew something was wrong. His clothes looked a little disheveled and his eyes were puffy, as if he had been crying. Evelyn thought something had happened at work.

"Babe, what's wrong?" she asked, wiping her hands on a dish towel and turning to face him.

Marcus didn't say anything for a moment, and Evelyn's intuition began to churn. She felt her face and chest start to get hot.

"What's wrong?" she asked again, bracing herself for what was to come.

He looked up and cleared his throat. "Can we talk upstairs?" He nodded toward the living room. "I don't want the kids to hear."

Slowly, Evelyn walked past him and up the stairs. She sat on the bed in their room and waited.

Marcus followed a few minutes later and leaned against the door frame. He rubbed the back of his neck and remained silent, wondering how to confess the truth.

"Marcus, you've got three seconds to tell me what's wrong, because you're freaking me out," Evelyn snapped.

He looked at her in the eye and finally spoke. "I messed up. I . . . slept with Tiffany last week."

Evelyn's head was spinning as she sat there, paralyzed. *Tiffany? His coworker? The woman who had smiled in her face at the annual holiday Christmas party for the past three years?* That *Tiffany?*

"Babe . . ." Marcus started.

She held up her hand to stop him from speaking and pointed at the closet. "You have five minutes to pack a bag and find someplace else to sleep tonight."

His face fell. "Ev —"

"Don't say anything else to me, Marcus. Don't act like I have to hear you out."

"If you could just let me explain . . ."

"There is nothing to talk about. Not now anyway."

Marcus's eyes looked glassy and Evelyn could tell that he was hurt by her refusal to listen to his explanation. *Good,* she thought to herself.

She pushed herself off the bed, grabbed an overnight bag from the bottom of the closet, and tossed it in Marcus' direction. Then she stepped past him without looking back. "Five minutes."

Marcus had indeed packed a bag that night and left, but over the following week, he wore Evelyn down with his constant calls, messages, and promises to do better by her in the future. "I've loved you for twelve years," he said in one voicemail. "I can't imagine the pain I've caused you. But I wanted to be honest. I wanted to let you know that I messed up. I take full responsibility. Can you please think about giving me another chance?"

Evelyn was reluctant. She had seen this play out in her parents' marriage. Her father had cheated on her mother and she took him back, committing herself to a life of looking over her shoulder. Evelyn didn't want to be the kind of woman a man could walk all over.

But she did miss him. And the kids missed him. They had a long history together and the good times in their marriage made her think that maybe, just maybe, it was possible that they could work it out.

Now, two months later, they were clinging to their marriage in weekly counseling sessions, trying to get to the bottom of what happened.

Just as Evelyn was about to suggest that they go ahead and get started, Marcus came into the room, apologizing profusely.

"There was traffic," he said, leaning over to give his wife a kiss. She stiffened as his lips touched her cheek.

Evelyn cleared her throat. "Things have been difficult at home. I am still struggling to even look at him. Every day that he goes to work, I'm wondering if he sees his co-worker and still has feelings for her or if this is really over. He swears to me that it is and I'm trying to believe him. But I still just don't know how I'm supposed to forgive him."

She looked over at Marcus, who was staring at a spot on the floor. She continued.

"I want to forgive him, but I don't think he understands how much this *hurts*. It feels like my heart has been ripped out. I want to go back to how it used to be. I want to trust him again—but is that even possible?"

Marcus didn't even wait for the counselor to jump in. "Babe, you know I love you. And I know I hurt you. That's why I'm here. To fix it. To make it right."

Evelyn just shook her head. "I don't even know if you can."

wHen lovInG you Is HurtInG Me

We've consulted many couples like Evelyn and Marcus, who are spinning in a world of hurt. They're unsure how to move forward and put the pieces of their marriage back together.

They're asking all the same questions you've probably asked yourself: *Why does this hurt so much? How can I move forward? Am I a fool if I decide to work this out?*

Whether you have sought the help of a professional therapist or are attempting to work through this fight on your own, we are here to help. Consider this book the next step on the path to healing.

In this chapter, we'll run through some of the most common issues we see couples struggling with. We believe there is power in telling the truth. Too often, we don't know how to make it through those dark times, because the people who have gone before us chose to keep quiet about what they went through. They don't want people in their business.

That's understandable. The work to heal your marriage is often a personal journey, which has you feeling raw and vulnerable. We also know that sharing what you've been through can be painful, as it dredges up old memories and puts your healing to the test.

But most of all, too many of us have been taught that we "keep family business in the house." We don't live in a culture of sharing every storm we've successfully navigated.

That's why we're the first ones to raise our hands and give our testimony. Being pastoral counselors with an increasingly visible profile, we want others to know that we're not just speaking about theories we've read, but that we've actually overcome challenges in our marriage as well. Each day, we're committing to the ministry of reconciliation right along with you.

We have been married for fifteen years. It has been an amazing ride, but don't think that we haven't weathered our fair share of storms. People often think that ministry marriages have fewer problems and struggles, but we've had to work through our own situations.

Our first hurdle arrived when our marriage was brand new. We found out that not only were we expecting a child — we were having twins.

Naomi was equal parts excited and scared — excited because she was thrilled to be expanding our family (to get pregnant successfully at thirty-eight is not always easy) and scared because whew, twins. Joel was excited and ready to meet his kids for the first time. We were ready.

The pregnancy was mostly uneventful. Naomi was happy because God had answered her prayers. Since she was becoming a first-time mother at a later age, she had prayed for twins. Easier to get the big family she wanted if we started out with two children!

When we brought them home, however, life had forever changed. Instantly, everything was different. Having twins meant that you had to do everything twice — feeding two babies, changing two diapers, rocking two babies to sleep. And getting them to do everything on the same schedule, that took months. It was a complete shock to the system. It was all hands on deck for a long time until we could get into a good rhythm with the kids.

On top of all those challenges, Naomi was dealing with body issues after giving birth to twins. As any woman who has carried a baby to term knows, your body changes in so many ways.

It wasn't until years later (well after we had our third child in 2005) that we realized we were having our own private storms. While we had turned toward each other for the first seven years of our marriage, something had shifted. (We'll discuss our biggest hurdle in more detail in chapter 5.)

Together, we worked through that situation and it helped strengthen us for other issues that may arise. Remember that conflict is inevitable in any relationship, but it's how you manage it that counts.

The Warning Signs

We believe that marriages do not just crumble overnight. What we think is the cause of a problem is often just the symptom. In our work with couples, we've noticed that there are usually signs of breakdown that occur before a family is shattered. We will list what we believe are the top three. If any of these three elements are prevalent in a marriage, you can be sure that trouble will soon follow:

- Breakdown in communication

- Breakdown in trust

- Breakdown in intimacy

Breakdown In Communication

Think back to the beginning of any relationship. Conversation flowed freely. It seemed like you would never run out of things to talk about. You were happy to see that person's name on your caller ID. Their voice was one of your favorite sounds in the world.

Fast-forward a few years into a relationship. Chances are the communication has turned from romance-driven conversations to mundane, task-driven conversations. There's less "Baby, what you got on?" and more "Did you remember to thaw out the chicken?"

With all the responsibilities that come with adulthood, sometimes we lose sight of where our communication should be. We forget to set aside time each day to sit face to face with zero distractions. We fall into a rut of thinking we know the other person so well that we don't need to continue to discover more about them. We begin to live life as roommates, not as lovers.

Usually this is one of the first cracks in a marriage. After all, if the communication between a couple remains strong, they are usually able to address issues as they arise, sort out a solution without the conversation getting too heated or personal, and then move on with the knowledge that both parties were heard. But when communication goes off the rails, sometimes couples won't even have those important conversations. Instead, issues get swept under the rug, piling up until one day someone trips.

In other cases, couples still communicate, but they've fallen out of habit of protecting their spouse with their words. Remember that Proverbs 18:21 tells us, "Death and life are in the power of the tongue: and they that love it shall eat the fruit thereof" (KJV). If we are not careful with the way we wield our words, we can find that they become weaponized.

As time goes on, sometimes we forget about the love. We don't act in the best interest of our marriage. We argue when we should remember that we're on the same team. We fight to be heard. We keep trying to "win," even though in a marriage, if one of you loses, then you both lose. We forget to "fight fair" and throw the rules out the window.

Is it any wonder, then, that we aren't as close as we used to be? Words are the lifeblood of any marriage, and if you are feeling constantly under attack, your marriage woes will grow into a life of their own.

If you are reading this and nodding your head, know that communication woes affect a majority of couples, and are typically one of the first things we notice when people come in to our offices. We did a survey of 130 couples in 2016, and a full sixty percent reported having communication issues.

If you think back to the months before your marriage was shattered, was communication a problem for the two of you? Did you find yourself growing apart and talking less and less? Or did your communication grow more charged and volatile?

In the following chapters, we will run down ways to engage in solid, strong communication, stronger than yesteryear. Trust us when we say that we have seen marriages have a full restoration in this department. It will take a bit of work and energy but with time, you can have a marriage full of good stuff.

Breakdown In trust

We might be showing our age a bit with this story, but do you remember in high school when they gave unassuming teenagers an egg for a week and asked them to pretend it was a baby? It was supposed to be a lesson on the responsibility of parenting, but we're not sure how effective it was. Students would leave their egg with a friend, crush it in their book bag or just leave it somewhere and forget about it.

Our relationships are like that egg. They are precious. You have to keep your eye on them and treat them with the utmost respect. If you stumble or otherwise act irresponsibly, you risk ruining a good thing. Once it is gone, it is extremely hard to get it back.

Why is trust so hard to rebuild? For one, humans have an excellent memory of pain. When it comes from our spouse, one person who is supposed to love and protect us, it sears even deeper into our memory bank. It's a biological protection, built in to help us avoid physical or emotional danger.

When we fell in love, we were raw and vulnerable. We had to be! Those strong feelings of love are only possible once you've opened your heart to let another person in. If they then betray you, your heart won't soon let you forget it.

We have struggled with trust in our relationship. No, we haven't had to deal with any sexual infidelity, but we have had to answer the question: "Do I believe you will act with my best interests at heart?" That's the basis of trust: "If I'm not around, will you do your best not to hurt me?" (We'll talk about that more in a later chapter.)

To rebuild trust, you have to take it one day at a time. Every day, you have to make a decision to get back in the fight and open yourself up to trust again, to be vulnerable again. This is why it's so important to reach out for help.

If your marriage is paralyzed by broken trust, keep reading for more. We're going to share how couples can rebuild trust and grow even deeper in their love.

Breakdown In Intimacy

We know what you're probably thinking—"breakdown in intimacy" really means "breakdown in sexual intimacy." But intimacy isn't just about sex. Intimacy is literally any act that creates deeper emotional and physical bonds between spouses. Sex is an important part of it, but so is date night, having meaningful conversations, and keeping the other person's love tank full.

Intimacy is something we see many couples focus on in the early stages of their relationships. They are very committed to date nights and quality time. They are quick to buy things for their partner that will make them smile. They listen when their partner has had a hard day and offer words of encouragement to cheer them up.

But with a few years under their belt, many couples begin to stray from having any type of curiosity about their partner. They don't yearn to have those long conversations anymore, they don't set aside time for dates, and yes, their sex life takes a dip.

This is where trouble can rear its ugly head. We rarely see a couple come to us when both parties have full love tanks. That's because there is no need! When both people are feeling loved and valued in the relationship (and that is due to strong intimacy), there's no fertile ground for conflict. When a person feels well loved, it's easier for them to give their partner the benefit of the doubt in an argument, hear their side, and be willing to compromise. If they are feeling neglected or unloved, all of that will go out the window.

There are so many reasons why intimacy decreases over time in a marriage, but two of the main ones are time and energy. The longer we're together, the more comfortable we get with each other. This can be a good and bad thing. It's a bad thing when we think that we no longer have to make our relationship the priority and feel comfortable setting it aside to focus on work, the kids, community obligations, etc.

All marriages will go through seasons of this, however. Naturally there will be times where you are closer and more intimate, but we all go through seasons where intimacy is missing and you're unsure when it's coming back.

Intimacy is what bonds us together. It's what we draw from when stress rears its ugly head and threatens to disrupt the status quo. Without a strong base of intimate behavior, we lose elasticity in our marriage. Instead of bending, we break.

But even if you feel the intimacy is gone (and has been for a while), you can get it back. We've consulted many couples on the brink, and we've witnessed total restoration in the area of intimacy. All hope is not lost.

How did We Get Here? and How do We Get Out?

What causes a marriage to be shattered? We can break it down into several different scenarios, but relationship expert John Gottman, co-founder of the Gottman Relationship Institute, points the finger at one reason — betrayal. "Betrayal is the secret that lies at the heart of every failing relationship," he says in his book, *What Makes Love Last.* "It is there even if the couple is unaware of it."[1]

We don't really have to describe what betrayal is, because for those living in its aftermath, it's not something you know, but something you feel. Infidelity, pornography addiction, and dishonesty are all forms of betrayal that can take a marriage down. Each of these comes with its own burdens, but at the heart of the matter, one spouse is feeling hurt and alone while the other is reeling from having caused their partner pain. It's a minefield of emotion. With the slightest trigger, you can find yourself back at square one, where the pain still feels fresh.

We started this chapter with Evelyn and Marcus's story because we know that the pain of infidelity rocks us to our core. It is one of the deepest forms of betrayal, and it takes a long-term commitment to get back on track after an affair. Yet despite this pain, both of them are looking for reconciliation, which has driven them to counseling. We have met many couples at this point in their marriage, and have walked hand-in-hand with them on the journey from broken to whole. We know it's not easy. But we know it works.

In each of the chapters to come, we will move through what we believe are the three steps to reconciliation. Here they are in brief:

- Reconciling with God

- Reconciling with ourselves

- Reconciling with our partners

It's important to note that you can't skip a step in this process. It would be tempting to go right to chapter 4 and try to begin working on your relationship.

But you're not there yet.

The secret to healing your marriage is that it begins with you, who were created in God's image. Often we rush to fix the relationship simply because it hurts so much. We want that quick fix. But rushing to repair the relationship without first going to the basics of who you are as one of God's children is simply putting a Band-Aid on the problem.

We aren't offering surface solutions. We're going to dive deep. Each step of the process is there for a reason, and we've seen it work firsthand. This is not an untested theory, but a biblical approach put into practice with hundreds of couples.

A final word of advice: All the marriage books and articles won't help if you aren't willing to do the work. It's not just about fixing what's broken in your marriage. If you do it right, you'll also be tackling what's broken in *you*.

Our marriages are designed to be a mirror. They show us who we really are. Our spouses hold up a light to our imperfections. There's a reason why they say, "Opposites attract." It's because through marriage, we see where we lack, whether it's patience, empathy or perseverance.

So roll up your sleeves.

Be prepared to see parts of yourself that you won't like. Be prepared to see parts of your *spouse* that you don't like – and then actively decide you'll love them anyway.

This is where maturity comes into play. It's about pushing through short-term discomfort for long-term gain. It's tempting to throw in the towel, to think that you aren't strong enough or built for this type of introspection. But you are. We've seen people walk through this process and exhale the biggest breath of their life once they realized that their marriage, while not perfect, was just right for them. They were actively healing.

There will be parts of this that challenge you so much that you must become a better person in order to carry out the mission. You can*not* remain self-centered and arrogant while doing this work. You have to shed everything that will get in the way.

Joel likes to say that marriage is one of the few areas of their lives where people balk at doing the hard work. People work hard on their finances and on their careers – they need to understand that their marriage is no different.

However, the reward is so incredibly great. It might be hard to imagine it now, but consider a future where you have the marriage of your dreams, where trust is restored, communication is easy and free-flowing, and you are having the time of your life.

That's what lies on the other side of the work — not perfection, but serenity. A confidence in the resilience of your marriage that will take you through anything else life has in store for you.

Chapter Two

Back To The Source
Reconciling With God

David looked over the menu and tried to think of something to say to Pam, his wife of five years. They had been struggling to communicate lately and he thought that going out to dinner, without their daughter, might give them a chance to reconnect.

But it didn't seem like Pam was interested. She sat stiffly across the booth and glanced around the restaurant, looking everywhere but at her husband.

"What are you going to order?" he asked, to break the silence.

Pam hadn't even opened her menu. "The grilled chicken."

"Are you sure? Because this place has great ribs. Remember that time I brought some home — "

"I'm sure," she interrupted. "I'll have the chicken."

David's shoulders slumped a bit. He took Pam's curt reply as his cue to leave her alone. He tapped his fingers on the cover of his menu and looked around at the other couples in the restaurant who were out trying to enjoy their Friday night.

By the window, there was a couple who were obviously on their first date. David remembered when Pam used to smile at him the way the woman was smiling at the man across from her.

It had been seven years since David and Pam had met at a networking event, after being introduced by a mutual friend. David wasn't interested in her at the time — he had a girlfriend — but took her information in case they could work together on a project in the future.

Pam wasn't really looking to be in a relationship either. She was a newly single mom raising a one-year-old daughter, and was concentrating on being the best mom she could. Dating, she thought, could wait a while. But something about David was charming. He was always respectful, and he took the time to get to know her as friends first. After his relationship went south, he began spending more time with Pam. They realized they had so much in common: they both went to HBCUs, they loved family, and they were big comedy fans. They were so compatible as friends that it seemed only natural to take the next step forward.

Once they got together, though, their relationship seemed to move in hyper speed. They were always together, either as a couple or as a threesome. David got along great with her daughter and was happy to serve as a father figure, since Pam's ex wasn't really in the girl's life. They got engaged after a year. Looking back, David wondered if they had moved too quickly, as now everything seemed on the brink of collapse.

A little over a year earlier, David's boss had called him into his office at the end of a long work day. "I'm sorry to have to do this to you," he said, "but your position has been terminated, effective immediately."

David cleaned out his office and dreaded having to tell his wife that he lost his job.

But to his surprise, Pam was calm and confident when he told her the news. "Hey, I'm sure you will find something else soon," she assured him. "And don't forget that I work too. I can carry us for a little while. Don't worry about it. You can sleep in tomorrow."

That lifted David's spirits for a bit, and he plunged himself into his job search. At first, it looked promising—he'd get called back for a second interview, only to be told they were going with the other candidate. Then he noticed he wasn't getting called back for as many second interviews. After about six months, it slowed down to where he was lucky to get any response at all.

To her credit, Pam did not nag him about his job search or ask him to take a lower-paying job just to help out with the bills. He remained in charge of the bills like always, and she hadn't seen any late notices or had any creditors calling, so she felt like she could hang in for a while longer.

But about five months into his unemployment, he noticed that she would scoot closer to the wall when he tried to spoon her in bed, and her excuse of "I'm too tired" became more and more frequent. It probably didn't help that when she left for work and when she came home, she found him on the same spot on the couch, scrolling through Facebook on his phone.

Now, his unemployment had ended (Pam didn't yet know), their savings account was tapped dry, and his severance money was long gone. David was starting to panic because money was tight and he didn't know how to tell his wife that what he was doing wasn't working. He needed to switch industries, salary targets, or something, because it was clear she was tired of being the only one bringing in money. Their budget couldn't take the strain much longer.

In truth, Pam was beyond tired. She had started working overtime on a new project and was also picking up the slack at home. David had begun sinking deeper into a depression and didn't really cook or clean anymore. They were barely speaking.

Realizing that the tension in their house could cut a knife, David had asked his brother for some money and used it to take his wife out to eat, an attempt to get out of the house and just enjoy life for a change without stressing about the bills piling up at home.

But it wasn't going well. They were picking at dinner, trying to figure out what to say to each other.

David cleared his throat. "How's your chicken?"

"It's fine," she said, pushing it around on her plate.

"Are you sure? You're not eating much."

"It's chicken, David. Same thing I get every time."

"You could have gotten something else," he said, his temper beginning to rise. He was trying to make it up to her, but attitude was all he was getting back.

Pam heard the annoyance in his voice and finally looked her husband in the eye. "I was trying to pick the cheapest thing, since we have to cut back now."

David sucked his teeth. "Is this why you have this attitude? Because things are tight right now?"

She rolled her eyes and put down her knife and fork. "I'm fine."

"Pam, you're obviously not fine," David said. "You won't talk to me. I don't know what else you want me to say."

Pam took a deep breath. "I don't know what you want *me* to say."

"Say something. Because obviously, you're holding something against me."

Pam didn't respond. She just picked up her fork and stuffed some of her chicken in her mouth. David sighed and pushed his plate away. He was no longer hungry.

They didn't say anything to each other the entire ride home.

When they got to their apartment, David grabbed the mail out of the mailbox and started going through it. A yellow envelope caught his eye.

He opened it quickly and his eyes scanned the page.

Pam noticed his uneasiness. "What is that?"

"Um . . . it's nothing. I'll take care of it." He tried to quickly stuff the letter back into the envelope but Pam was too quick. She read the heading.

"'Notice to Evict'?" she said, dumbfounded. "What in the world is this?"

"We've fallen behind a bit, but it's nothing. I'll get this straightened out tomorrow." David reached for the paper but Pam held it just out of reach.

"How did this happen?" she asked, still in shock. "Tell me the truth. I've been giving you my paycheck for the past six months. That plus your unemployment should have gotten us through."

"My unemployment ended two months ago," he admitted, rubbing the back of his neck with his hand. "I was too embarrassed to tell you."

"Too embarrassed? So how embarrassing is it going to be when the three of us are sleeping in a cot at the homeless shelter." She threw the paper on the kitchen table and turned on her heels to stomp into the living room.

David followed behind, full of regret. "I'm sorry, Pam. But I promise I'll get this fixed."

"Why did you let it get so bad without telling me? We're supposed to be a team."

"I was hoping I could fix it before you found out."

"And then you took me to dinner tonight knowing the bills haven't been paid? Who does that?"

"I just wanted us to have some fun together. We've been so stressed lately."

"Yes, David. We've been stressed because there is no *money*."

David decided to stop talking. He knew there was nothing he could really say in this situation. They were facing eviction and he wasn't sure how he was going to get them out of this. He knew his best bet would be to let Pam say her piece and then get to work on a solution.

"You're going to have to ask your dad for the money," she said finally.

"I can't do that," he said.

"What?" she said, stunned. "Why not?"

"Because they're old. They need their money."

"David, your family is about to be on the *street*. I'm sure they won't mind giving us money so that won't happen."

"I can figure something out," David said firmly. "We don't need their help."

Pam rolled her eyes. "I'll ask my parents then."

"Pam . . ."

"I'm doing what I have to do," Pam said. Her voice did not waver. "I cannot wait on you to get us out of the mess you got us into. You have a family now. If there's something you can't handle, you're supposed to let me know. And you didn't. So my trust in your ability to 'figure it out' is gone."

after tHe trust Is Gone

The big issue with David and Pam comes down to trust. Remember we said that trust is a simple question: "Will you do your best not to harm me?"

In this relationship, and in many others we've seen, the erosion of trust is the source of the conflict to follow. Once you no longer believe your spouse will act in the best interest of the marriage, you know you have work to do.

So how do you fix it? We'll first share a quick story.

A couple years ago, our neighbor's house caught fire when they were trying to deep fry their Thanksgiving turkey in the garage (we probably could have told them that was a bad idea). The whole garage and left side of their house went up in flames.

Luckily, the fire department responded quickly and no one was hurt. Their home, however, was a mess. Both the interior and exterior were deeply damaged, and the necessary repairs were extensive. They had to move out of their home for six months, staying in a nearby apartment while the restoration was completed. First, they had to remove all the damaged pieces — the charred siding, the drywall, the gutters. Then they had to rebuild the parts of the house that had been compromised in the fire — structures that weren't even immediately visible but gave stability to the entire house.

Every day, we would see a little progress on the home. Little by little, it began to look like it did before. In the end, because they had done so much work on it, the house actually looked *better* than before the fire.

This is the key — they couldn't just air out the house and repaint everything without doing the foundational work first. Did they want to uproot their lives while the repair was taking place? We're sure they didn't. Was it comfortable living in a tiny apartment without most of the things they held dear to them? No, it wasn't. But it was necessary if they wanted to get back to their home.

Similarly, we want couples to understand that the first step in reconciliation has nothing to do with your partner. It's tempting to want to begin the process there, to begin with the actual person who is stuck in the conflict with you. But if you start there, you miss the opportunity to dig deep and build a new, solid foundation.

It might be uncomfortable to sift through the rubble, to see that your marriage wasn't as strong as you thought it was. But the only way out is *through*. You have to go *through* the damage in order to fix it.

WHat Is reConCIlatIon?

When we talk about reconciliation, we aren't simply talking about forgiving and forgetting. We're talking about *restoration*. Reconciliation is the restoration of friendly relations. It's the act of getting two parties back on the same page. It's deeper than simply saying, "I'm sorry." It's the full process through which we will be made new.

Our approach to the ministry of reconciliation in marriage came to Naomi as a divine inspiration from God. He put this message in her heart several years ago, and we have been walking with couples through it ever since.

It all springs from 2 Corinthians 5:16-20, the Scripture that gives us the blueprint for a lasting reconciliation:

> *So from now on we regard no one from a worldly point of view. Though we once regarded Christ in this way, we do so no longer. Therefore, if anyone is in Christ, the new creation has come: The old has gone, the new is here! All this is from God, who reconciled us to himself through Christ and gave us the ministry of reconciliation: that God was reconciling the world to himself in Christ, not counting people's sins against them. And he has committed to us the message of reconciliation. We are therefore Christ's ambassadors, as though God were making his appeal through us. We implore you on Christ's behalf: Be reconciled to God. God made him who had no sin to be sin for us, so that in him we might become the righteousness of God. (NIV)*

These verses are what we use when we begin the process with couples. Let's break down the three major points:

> *"Therefore, if anyone is in Christ, the new creation has come: The old has gone, the new is here!"*

This gives us the promise that we can be made new. We don't have to simply live in the hurt forever. There is a path forward and it begins with Christ. God tells us that the old is gone. That means we can let go of the pain, and we can rest in His promise that we don't have to suffer under those old hurts. We can be forward focused instead of living life looking in the rearview mirror.

> *"All this is from God, who reconciled us to himself through Christ and gave us the ministry of reconciliation."*

As Naomi likes to say, if God could reconcile the world to Himself, then that means none of our problems are insurmountable. Isn't that powerful? That gives us the confidence to go forward and tackle our issues with the knowledge that we can succeed. It's all possible. We don't have to worry that we won't be able to solve our problems, because God already proved that we will be victorious.

> *". . . that God was reconciling the world to himself in Christ, not counting people's sins against them."*

We'll talk more about forgiveness in an upcoming chapter, but the most important part here is "not counting people's sins against them." We're all human, which means we are predisposed to remembering what and who have harmed us. But letting go of old hurts promises us a more fruitful future. This takes practice, and we're here to help you thrive in it. After all, forgiveness is as much for you as it is for your spouse.

Quality tIMe wItH God

Even as pastoral counselors, we can admit that we sometimes stray in our relationship with God. When our days fill up with various adult responsibilities, we sometimes find ourselves giving God what's left of us.

Shattered

So the first step in reconciliation is to reconcile with God.

That means making sure that God is the center, because that relationship with God is the foundation of everything else you will do. We are *of* God, meaning if we are aligned with Him and His Word, there is nothing we can't do. If we have found that we have strayed, we simply have to get back to the source.

The quickest way to do that is to seek quality time with God. Our relationship with Him is like any other relationship — what you water will grow. You water your relationship with God by going to Him in prayer.

Give God all your hurt. Let Him see you as you really are. You don't have to hide anything in this relationship. God indeed knows your heart. Give Him access to you and let Him work to help you feel whole again.

As Naomi always says, "We don't have to put on a show. We just have to be honest." When we want to grow closer with God, all you have to do is talk to Him. Having those conversations brings trust and intimacy.

So where do you begin these discussions? We're pastoral counselors and we guide people by using Scripture, biblical principles, prayer, and other theoretical techniques:

> *"For God so loved the world that he gave his one and only Son, that whoever believes in him shall not perish but have eternal life." John 3:16 (NIV)*

This Scripture tells us everything we need to know: God loves us. The late great Maya Angelou once had a segment on Oprah Winfrey's show where she cried thinking of how great God's love is. "It still humbles me," she said through tears, "That this force that made leaves and fleas and stars and rivers and you ... loves me. Me, Maya Angelou. It's amazing. I can do anything and do it well. Any good thing, I can do it. That's why I am who I am. Yes. Because God loves me and I'm amazed at it and grateful for it."

As husband and wife, we know how deeply we love each other. But it's no comparison to the love God has for us. This verse is just further evidence to say, we have to get back to the beginning, because this is the best example of what love is.

> *"But God demonstrates his own love for us in this: While we were still sinners, Christ died for us." Romans 5:8 (NIV)*

The key phrase is "while we were *still* sinners." God doesn't ask for us to come to Him perfect and ready-made. He walks with us during our journey and loves us with all of our flaws. We sin daily, accidentally and on purpose, and that love doesn't go away. It is the greatest love any of us will ever know, and to walk in it is to feel a comfort like no other. He didn't wait for us to confess our belief in Him; He extended Himself to us before we even had Him on our mind. He did it while we were in our worst state. Can you imagine that type of love?

> *". . . because, if you confess with your mouth that Jesus is Lord and believe in your heart that God raised him from the dead, you will be saved. For with the heart one believes and is justified, and with the mouth one confesses and is saved." Romans 10:9-10 (ESV)*

If you look at the Bible, God actually asks very little of us. He knows who and what He created. He knows that human nature is sinful and flawed. He asks that we believe and have faith in Him and His word. That's the basis of all Christianity: to have faith. Faith is the belief in things unseen and unproven. That can only strengthen you as you fight to reconcile and build in your marriage.

". . . you have abandoned the love you had at first. Remember therefore from where you have fallen; repent, and do the works you did at first." Revelation 2:4-5 (ESV)

Relationships are work, and in the midst of working to maintain our lives and our loves, we can work God right out of the picture. This is when we must be intentional about putting God first and reprioritizing our lives.

As you sit with and work through these Scriptures, consider joining a Bible study group to help you get the most out of your readings. Having prayer warriors walk beside you on your journey can also help you feel like you're not doing the work alone.

fIll tHe VoId

What we tend to do in a marriage relationship is to expect our spouse to fulfill all our needs. Isn't that what most marriage vows say? They are supposed to be there for us, through hell and high water, through sickness and health, for richer or poorer.

We go into marriage thinking it's going to be the ultimate twosome. When we're low, they'll pull us up, and vice versa.

But the truth is that our spouses are only human. If you expect them to be perfect, that will surely lead to disappointment. You have to understand that your spouse is a fallible human being. Because you are married to another human being, you need to look to God to have those voids filled.

This was a lesson we both had to learn early in our marriage. As Naomi will tell couples we work with, "One of the biggest errors I made during those early years was that I expected Joel to be there any time I was lonely or needed reassurance. But he's a human being with his own limitations."

Then Joel will usually add, "I like to joke with my wife that I'm not Jesus, Jr. Sometimes I didn't understand what type of comfort she needed or how she needed it. And she felt disappointed."

This is why you have to learn how to be still and let God fill those voids. For some of us, this might not be second-nature, but we have to train ourselves to turn to God. It would be nice if our spouse could *always* give us the emotional support and validation we seek, but they are only human.

Reconciling with God is about getting everything else off the shelf that we may have placed before God. It is coming back to having God as the center. When we can get back to this relationship with God, all other restoration will flow from that. When we're in a relationship with God, we can see ourselves through God's eyes. That perspective, nurture, and freedom can't come from our spouse. Our spouses are not equipped to handle that. They don't have that divine power to liberate us.

But here's the best part: your relationship with God is one of the purest forms of love you will experience. There is a serenity that washes over you once you realize that God is looking out for you and only wants the best for you. It's a relationship you can count on through everything.

It's truly a two-way relationship. You can hear God speak to you through His text. Spending time with the Word reinforces the promises He has made. You can rest in the knowledge that yes, God's got you.

Chapter Three

Digging Deep
Reconciling With Ourselves

Denise pulled her phone from her pocket and dashed off a quick email to her boss. She was running late after dropping the kids off at school and daycare, and she didn't want him to hold up the meeting waiting for her. The previous week at work had been crazy, and even though it was only Monday, she could tell this week was getting off to a rocky start as well.

Her husband Charles had forgotten to mention that he had an early morning meeting and, as usual, dashed off before she could remind him that *she* had an early meeting as well. She was trying to take it in stride, as she knew he was up for a promotion and had a lot of extra stress on his plate. But she couldn't help feeling a little resentment for what she saw as thoughtlessness — for her and her career.

They had been fighting through a rocky period in their marriage, with their conversations getting shorter and shorter and more often only about the kids. She tried to think of the last time he had complimented her and was ashamed to think of the last time she had complimented him. Their seven-year wedding anniversary had passed last week and they hadn't even celebrated. Charles worked late, and Denise didn't feel like reminding him about it, trying to avoid another argument. When he finally remembered the next day, he sent her a quick text apology: *Sorry about yesterday. Just got a lot on my mind at work.*

Denise focused on the road ahead, trying to make it to work relatively close to her usual time. When she finally made it to the office twenty minutes late, she was surprised to see a cup of coffee on her desk. As she shrugged out of her coat, her co-worker Marvin poked his head in.

"Hey superstar," he said with a big grin on his face. He strolled in the office and sat in one of the two chairs facing her desk. "Davis said you'd be running a little late so I got you a latte. I know they're your favorite."

"Aw, thanks," Denise said, sitting down at her desk and taking a big sip. "Man, it's the perfect temperature and everything."

"I asked them to make it extra hot so it would keep until you got here," he said with a big grin.

Denise simply smiled back and clutched the cup between her hands, allowing its warmth to spread to her fingers. "Well, thank you. That was so thoughtful of you."

"Just looking out," Marvin said with a shrug. "You better hustle down to Davis' office to get the update on our new client. It looks like we're going to be pulling a lot of overtime with this one."

Denise groaned. The last thing she needed was an ultra-demanding new client.

"I'll go ahead and get out your hair," he said, rising to leave. "See you for lunch?"

"Oh, yes. I'll meet you by the elevators."

Since Denise had begun working at her new advertising firm three years ago, she had found a real friend in Marvin. They had gone to the same college and grew up in the same area of Chicago. He often joked with her that they were probably just walking past each other their whole lives, never knowing they were in the same rooms.

But what really cemented their relationship as work colleagues was when Denise went out on maternity leave. Marvin had sent her weekly emails about what was going on in the office and had made sure to bring her up in staff meetings so people wouldn't forget her contributions while she was out with the baby. Her career was important to her, so it was kind of Marvin to make sure she didn't fall behind during her three-month leave.

After she got back, they started having lunch together every Monday, a great way to kick off the week and prepare herself for the endless onslaught of emails, meetings, and pitches. They spent a full hour laughing and joking about co-workers and difficult clients. It was one of the few times during Denise's busy week that she didn't feel like she had to do anything for anybody else. She could just be herself and relax.

Her husband Charles had met Marvin once or twice at the holiday parties, but she hadn't made a big deal out of his presence in her life. He was her co-worker—nothing more, nothing less. She didn't want Charles to get into overprotective man mode and start problems where there weren't any. Besides, Marvin usually kept a rotation of women on speed dial and they usually spent half their Monday lunches talking about the crazy exploits he had gotten into the weekend before.

Still, Denise found herself more and more conflicted as time went on. All their inside jokes and lunches were harmless, right? Denise was trying hard to advance in a male-dominated field. *I need good co-workers who have my back in order to get ahead*, she convinced herself.

She finished her early morning work and gathered her things to meet Marvin for lunch. They usually hit up the Italian restaurant a few blocks over for lunch-close enough to walk but far enough that they didn't have to worry about their co-workers overhearing their conversations.

On the walk over, Marvin seemed to have something on his mind.

"You okay?" Denise asked. "You're really quiet today."

Marvin smiled weakly. "I'm fine."

"You sure?"

"Yeah." He nodded. "It's just . . . well, Ray said something as I was headed to meet you."

Ray was one of the senior partners at the firm and a notorious gossip. Until she met him, Denise didn't realize men could gossip even more than women did. Now she kept her guard up whenever he was around and did her best to make sure her name was never present in his casual conversations. "What did he say?" Denise asked.

"He was just making jokes," Marvin said. "Like, 'Oh, you're going to have lunch with your wife today?'"

"What?" Denise stopped walking.

"No, come on, I'm hungry," Marvin said, laughing. He stopped and tugged her arm, urging her to continue. She kept walking.

"And he was talking about me and you?" she asked, suddenly very self-conscious about their Monday tradition.

Marvin nodded. "Yeah, but it's fine. I told him we're just colleagues and our lunches are purely professional. Nothing to worry about."

Denise couldn't help thinking that maybe she *should* be worried. It was one thing to have a great co-worker, but quite another to consider that it was affecting her professional reputation.

They got their usual booth and looked over the menu, even though they got the same thing every time: Marvin, a Caesar salad with grilled chicken, and Denise, the chicken *piccata*.

Once they had placed their orders, Marvin leaned back against the cool leather. "So, you want to talk about what Ray said?"

"Yeah," Denise said, fiddling with her napkin.

"Figured as much." He took a deep breath. "You think we should stop our lunches?"

"I don't know." She sipped her water and looked at him. "What do you think?"

"I think that I like you a lot and I like our lunches. So, no, I don't want to stop because of what one guy said. It was a joke."

"That one guy is *your* boss. My boss," Denise reminded him. "And you're the one who told me about it, which means it must have bothered you a little."

"Well, maybe it did bother me a little. But I value our friendship. And if your own husband doesn't have a problem with it, then what's the big deal?"

Denise fell silent. Marvin knew her well enough to pick up on her discomfort.

"Wait, Charles knows about our lunches, right?" Marvin asked, leaning forward to look her in the eye.

She didn't answer.

"Denise?"

She sighed. "No, he doesn't know."

"Why not?"

"Marvin, I knew you wouldn't understand this because you're single. You don't have to be accountable to anybody. You come and go as you please. But me? I have to be careful. I don't want my husband getting the wrong idea."

Now it was Marvin's turn to be silent. "What would he get the wrong idea about? Do you think we've crossed a line?"

Denise took a deep breath. "I mean, we flirt sometimes."

"Yeah." Marvin grinned. "We do."

"And I don't know. Maybe I like the attention."

Suddenly, Denise didn't feel good. Everything about their weekly lunches, their familiarity, the fact that Marvin knew her favorite coffee order . . . it all felt too intimate.

Marvin excused himself to go to the bathroom. Denise took a deep breath and pulled out her phone. She knew she needed to come clean.

She sent a quick message to her husband: *Can we talk tonight?*

yearnInG to fIll tHe VoId

Living day by day in a shattered marriage can take a toll on you personally. It can make you do things you wouldn't normally do and say things you wouldn't ordinarily say. It can also make you vulnerable to outside temptations.

What do you do when your relationship is strained and you're yearning for everything to be like it was before? That lack of intimacy that we discussed in chapter 1 makes it easy for your attention to wander elsewhere.

As with Denise, emotional affairs are often the result of attempting to fill a void missing from your relationship. We see these often with our clients, as it's an easy slope to fall down. Denise and Marvin may have started out innocently enough, but during their relationship a line had been crossed. The fact that Denise felt she couldn't tell her husband about their weekly lunches was a red flag that something deeper was going on, even if she wasn't ready to admit it yet.

While you may not be dealing with infidelity (emotional or otherwise) in your relationship, you are probably still dealing with a lack of intimacy that allowed whatever shattered your marriage — dishonesty, financial strain, pornography addiction, etc. — to occur.

Part two of the ministry of reconciliation is reconciling with yourself. Once a marriage is shattered, you have to get back to the source — God — and then move on to the next person who can heal the situation: you.

Again, it's not yet time to focus on the relationship itself. It's still far too premature to think about healing the marriage. We have to work on ourselves first.

Take Denise. She and Charles were suffering from a lack of communication. Denise wasn't comfortable enough in her marriage to voice her concerns and felt more like a roommate than a cared-for spouse. This led to her finding comfort in the presence of another. Even though her relationship with Marvin was never physical, it definitely crossed a line between strictly platonic and into the area of romantic affection. The next step for Denise, and for any of us who find ourselves in this situation, is to ask ourselves some hard questions, beginning with the basic one: "What is it that I really need?"

WHo are you?

A popular ritual in modern weddings is the lighting of the unity candle. In this ritual, the bride and groom light their individual candles and use their respective flames to light a singular candle, representing their union. They then blow out their individual candles and allow the flame from their joint candle to shine.

We find it amazing that right at the beginning, there is symbolism that our individual selves must die in order for our marriages to thrive. This is just untrue. We tell couples all the time, "Don't blow out your candle!" Yes, we must be focused on building and strengthening our marital union, but it is crucial that we maintain our individual identities. What you bring to the relationship — your dreams, your goals, your vision — matters.

Throughout our marriage, there have been times when we are overwhelmed by responsibility and our individual needs have to fight to be heard. This is often what we see when we consult couples who are living their own shattered nightmare. Somewhere along the line, they have allowed who they are to be absorbed into the marriage.

Now they have to do the hard work to answer one question: "Who am I?"

We get into trouble when we lean so far into our marriages that we forget who we are. We forget to nourish the singular soul that resides within and allow ourselves to wither, in service of our marriage. You can't figure out what you want out of your marriage and your life if you don't first know who you are.

The road back to ourselves doesn't happen overnight. It takes time and lots of effort to get back to your full self.

So how do you rediscover yourself?

GoInG BaCk to tHe Word

You'll find in this book that whenever we have a question, we will always turn to His Word to give us clarity. Our quest to bring us back to ourselves leads us to Psalm 139:14:

> *I will praise thee; for I am fearfully and wonderfully made: marvellous are thy works; and that my soul knoweth right well.*

Read that again: "We are fearfully and wonderfully made." God took His time with us. We are His masterpieces. He looks at us and is proud to see who we are. Joel likes to say, "When God made us, He didn't make no junk!" God's works aren't just good or "okay." They are *marvelous*. God is the master craftsman. We have to remember that we are created in God's image, which means we are all beautiful and powerful in our own way. Remind yourself that you are one of God's children.

For our readers who are parents, you know firsthand the love that exists between a parent and child. There's nothing your child can do to sever that love. It is one of the purest forms of unconditional love that we can experience.

Now when we remember that we are God's children, that He loves us and wants the best for us in the same way that we do with our own children, doesn't that make you feel blessed?

In the following sections, we are going to hone in on this idea. We want you to understand that you are worthy of the love you're seeking. You deserve to have a love that mirrors Christ's love for the church. God's love for us can and will manifest itself in your marriage, but only if you know that you are worthy.

For women especially, problems in your marriage may trickle over into your feelings about yourself. Thoughts about your marriage might become all-consuming — you may spend your day at work mulling over last night's argument and dreading the fact that you have to go home to a house that's rife with tension. When your marriage is not right, it's harder to see all the other things in your life that *are* right.

This chapter is about focusing on yourself because you only have control over *you*. You can't force your spouse to change or apologize. You can't make them see the situation from your perspective. You can't make them agree with you. All you can do is handle your response to the situation.

This requires that we look inward and deal with whatever is weighing us down, whether it's immaturity, selfishness, control issues, or worse. We didn't come to this marriage as a perfect person, so whether you believe the issues in your marriage are your fault or not, there is still work that can be done on your end, even if it's just warming your heart up to the idea of forgiveness.

Author Gary Thomas, whose book *Sacred Marriage* is a staple in our premarital counseling sessions, argues that marriage is not about personal fulfillment, but a call to meet our higher selves.

"If I really wanted to see God transform me from the inside out," he writes in *Sacred Marriage*. "I'd need to concentrate on changing *myself* than on changing my *spouse.*"[1]

Couples who come to see us for consultation often focus outwardly. They want to make their partner see how much they're hurting. They want their partner to change whatever behavior is causing the problems in their marriage. Above all, they want to be heard and respected.

The best way to see a change in your marriage is to begin with yourself — and not just so you can have an amazing marriage, but be your best you just for you.

We tend to focus on the other person because that's what's comfortable. We often don't stop to think about our role in our marriage problems. But it's a sign of maturity to say to yourself, "This is where I can improve." This doesn't mean that if the other person betrayed you, that it's your fault. It's just about focusing on your behavior because you can't control anyone else.

It's about adhering to the principles of the serenity prayer: "God, grant me the serenity to accept the things I cannot change, the courage to change the things I can and the wisdom to know the difference."

Don't let the stress in your marriage make you hard or bitter. Don't let the problems you have with your spouse suck out all the joy in your life. We know it can make you feel like you're stuck, especially if you're someone who truly believes in the institution of marriage. If you're stuck in an unhappy marriage and you can't see the light at the end of the tunnel, it can be a very miserable experience. Who wants to think they've made a mistake?

Our advice is to make sure you're shedding the weight of the past. Become more future-focused and allow for more opportunities to affirm yourself. You want to remember who you are and *whose* you are.

Shattered

tHe power of affIrMatIons

When you take a hit in such a critical area of your life, often your self-esteem will suffer. After all, a big part of your identity is probably wrapped up in your role as a spouse. If you aren't doing well in that area, it's human nature to feel down on yourself and beat yourself up for not being smarter or not making better decisions. You'll spend so much of your mental energy stewing in your misery that you forget to esteem yourself.

We urge you to get clear on one thing: you are not the problems in your marriage. You are a vibrant person outside of your title of wife or husband.

What better time to focus inward than when you're struggling in one of your most valued relationships? The temperature is just right for loving so gently on yourself.

You want to bathe in self-love, reminding yourself that you are so worthy of all the good things in life. Look in the mirror and talk to yourself like you'd talk to your best friend. It might feel weird, but get in the habit of loving yourself from head to toe. Tell yourself, "My hands are strong and lovely, my legs are long and shapely, my mind is brilliant." Speak powerful words over yourself and see how quickly God will work to restore you.

If you need a place to start, here are some Bible verses to help you with your affirmations:

The Lord appeared to him from far away. I have loved you with an everlasting love; therefore I have continued my faithfulness to you. Jeremiah 31:3 (ESV)

So God created human beings in his own image. In the image of God he created them; male and female he created them. Genesis 1:27 (NLT)

41

You are altogether beautiful, my love; there is no flaw in you. Song of Solomon 4:7 (ESV)

[I pray] that according to the riches of his glory he may grant you to be strengthened with power through his Spirit in your inner being, so that Christ may dwell in your hearts through faith – that you, being rooted and grounded in love, may have strength to comprehend with all the saints what is the breadth and length and height and depth, and to know the love of Christ that surpasses knowledge, that you may be filled with all the fullness of God. Ephesians 3:16-19 (ESV)

For I am convinced that neither death, nor life, nor angels, nor rulers, nor things present, nor things to come, nor powers, nor height, nor depth, nor anything else in all creation, will be able to separate us from the love of God in Christ Jesus our Lord. Romans 8:38-39 (NIV)

SettInG Boundaries

Part of the reason we lose ourselves in our marriages is that we lack clear boundaries. We give and give and wonder why we come up empty. We're supposed to be filled and give from our overflow. How can we take care of anyone else if we don't have anything else?

Your boundaries are like fences. If you don't have a fence around your yard, any and everyone can come in to your personal space as they please. People could wear down your lawn, let their dogs relieve themselves on your grass, or toss junk in your yard.

But with a fence, you are better able to protect what's yours. This doesn't mean you build a ten-foot tall brick fence that no one can scale. No, your fence allows for some negotiation, like a wooden fence with a door to let people in as necessary.

Boundaries are great in marriage, because they allow you to keep some of yourself *for* yourself. Boundaries signal to another person, "This is where you end and I begin." In marriage, there's a temptation to dissolve all your boundaries. After all, this is supposed to be one of the most intimate relationships humans can have with each other. In the book *Boundaries in Marriage*, the authors Cloud and Townsend write that boundaries can be just the thing that can make your marriage feel brand new. "Often, when a crisis . . . occurs," they write, "it helps the struggling couple reconcile and remake their marriage into a more biblical one."[2]

As we mentioned earlier in the chapter with our unity candle example, we are still two individuals in this union. No matter how long you have been married or known each other, you are still two separate people with your individual needs and boundaries.

How do you know if you need better boundaries? Anger and energy are good starting points.

Do you frequently feel angry and can't quite pinpoint why that is? Chances are there are some boundaries being crossed that you have been unable to enforce. You've felt like people have been taking advantage of you and it's time for that to stop.

If you're feeling exhausted, like you have nothing left to give at the end of the week, you might need better boundaries, too. Good boundaries protect you and allow you to thrive. Without them, people will take what they want from you and if they don't hear you say stop, they will keep taking. What you allow is what will continue.

In formulating your boundaries, again recognize that you cannot control another person. Boundaries are about protecting *you* and your mental, physical, and emotional health.

Boundaries work best in the "If, then" format. *If* a person decides to do something you find offensive or doesn't otherwise sit well with you, *then* you will take whatever action you have decided is best.

Here's an example: if you don't like the way your spouse raises their voice at you during an argument, you can ask them to stop. But you truly don't have control over whether they listen to you and lower their volume. So your boundary may sound like this: "If you continue to yell while we try to have a discussion, I will leave and go into another room until we can have a conversation without the yelling."

It takes practice to set boundaries and enforce them. When other people first encounter boundaries where you previously had none, you will face some pushback. But you will have to be firm, as you know that you are doing this for *you*.

fidelity vs. Infidelity

In helping you put a shattered marriage back together, we'd be remiss if we didn't talk about fidelity. While your marriage may not be recovering from infidelity (emotional or otherwise), fidelity is still a topic we feel doesn't get enough attention until it's too late.

Another way to think of fidelity is loyalty. When it comes to rebuilding your marriage, you need to take a good long look at your commitment. Are you easily swayed and frustrated by the day to day ups and downs of marriage? Are you always mentioning divorce or separation at the slightest hiccup? A large part of fidelity is to understand that you signed up for the long run. Marriage is a consistent investment into the life of another. It's about your spouse acting as sandpaper, gently and consistently sanding down your rough edges and bringing forth your true potential.

With that in mind, you have to make a decision. Are you in or are you out? If you are in, then you have to do what it takes to stay in this.

forGIveness

Who do you have to forgive?

As you take the steps to heal yourself, recognize that your true work won't be done until you can release the pain you've been holding on to . . . and forgive.

Author and therapist Terry Gaspard, a frequent contributor to marriage sites, including the Gottman Institute, says that forgiveness is less about the person who has hurt you and more about granting yourself freedom. "It is about choosing to live a life wherein others don't have power over you and you're not dominated by unresolved bitterness and resentment."[3]

Forgiveness is an ultimate act of self-love, because it allows you to move toward a fuller, happier future where you are not bogged down by the realities of your past.

A quick clarification on forgiveness. We often hear the phrase "forgive and forget." In reality, however, we don't need to forget what has happened to us. As we mentioned in the introduction, forgiveness resembles *Kintsukuroi* — the Japanese art of repairing broken ceramics with golden lacquer. It's not about forgetting what has happened, but choosing to see it as a part of your past that challenged you, but didn't break you. After all, we can't go back and erase the past, but we can look forward to a brighter future. That's only possible if you forgive.

Fred Luskin, one of the foremost experts on forgiveness, puts it this way: Forgiveness is giving up all hope for a better past.

"Forgiveness allows you a fresh start, whether it's a big insult or a small one," he said in a PBS interview. "It's like a rain coming to a polluted environment. It clears things. At some point, you can say that this awful thing happened to me. It hurt like hell, yet I'm not going to allow it to take over my life. That's the choice that's always available."[4]

Forgiveness is a choice. It may not always feel like it, but you can choose it at any time, whenever you're ready.

At this point, you must begin to forgive yourself. Not just for the sake of your marriage, but for you. You deserve that release.

I forgive myself for what I didn't know.

I forgive myself for any harm I have caused myself or others.

I forgive myself for the times I did not always act with the heart of a servant.

I forgive myself for acting solely in my best interest.

Chapter Four

Finding Your Way Back
Reconciling To Each Other

evelyn and MarCus

Marcus pulled into the driveway and took a deep breath. Things had been shaky between him and his wife since he confessed to having an affair with one of his co-workers, Tiffany, six months ago. Every conversation seemed like it opened a fresh wound. Marcus wasn't sure if he could ever handle seeing his wife cry so much. Every tear felt like a punch to the gut.

As he walked in the front door, he could hear the kids playing upstairs and was grateful that he might be able to talk to his wife alone for a few minutes at least. She was sitting at the kitchen table, sorting the mail. When he came into view in the kitchen, she looked up at him for a moment, gave him a half-smile and turned her attention back to the mail.

This was pretty much the reaction Marcus had anticipated. She had thawed a bit toward him, thanks to biweekly therapy sessions, but they were still so far from where they had once been. The only good thing he could say is that they were now able to be in the same room without an argument popping off — most of the time. *That's progress*, he thought to himself.

Months earlier, when Marcus had noticed his co-worker Tiffany flirting a little too heavily with him, he was shocked. He didn't

47

realize he could still attract the attention of young, beautiful women like her. He knew he wasn't ugly, but since settling down with a wife and kids, women rarely paid him any attention. It was almost like he was invisible.

He also felt invisible inside his own home too. His life with Evelyn was fine, if a little boring. They were comfortable with each other. For the most part, Marcus thought he wasn't really missing anything. They were busy with the kids and growing their careers, and they felt okay putting their relationship on the backburner.

When he went out of town on a business trip and ended up in the same hotel as Tiffany, he honestly didn't have any intention on stepping out on Evelyn. He was almost as shocked as anybody when he woke up in Tiffany's hotel room, sweaty and ashamed.

He knew right away that he had to tell Evelyn what had happened, but he feared losing everything important to him. He knew Evelyn would be well within her rights to leave him and he was terrified of facing the music.

He mulled it over for a week before deciding to just come right out with it, like ripping off a Band-Aid. The sooner he told her, the sooner they could face what would come next. He knew living a lie wasn't an option.

After she initially threw him out, he begged and pleaded for her to give him another chance. Now, six months later, they were on speaking terms, but the warmth and love he had previously taken for granted was nowhere to be found.

He had taken steps to make sure Evelyn knew she could trust him again. He requested a transfer to a different branch so he wouldn't be passing Tiffany in the hallways every day. He came straight home after work, turning down his friends' Thursday night invitations to watch the game at a local bar. He started taking on more responsibility in the house, doing the laundry and making sure the kitchen was always stocked. He started writing weekly letters to his wife, telling her how much he loved her and how much he wanted things to work.

Still, he knew it was going to take time to win her back. She had let him back in the house, but not back into her heart. When his friends started complaining that he never left the house anymore, he simply replied, "I've got to make this right. I'm in it for as long as it takes."

Evelyn was impressed by Marcus's new commitment, but she wasn't ready to completely forgive. She was thankful that Marcus was demonstrating how he was re-committed to the marriage, but thanks to some great advice from their marriage counselor, she had taken this time to *not* focus on her marriage, but to focus on herself.

She started thinking about where things had gone wrong, and reluctantly she began to see that the cracks in what she thought was a strong marriage were there all along. The biggest one? Somewhere along the line she had stopped thinking of herself as "Evelyn" and more like "Marcus's wife and mother of his kids."

When did I lose myself? she wondered. She decided that she would let Marcus do whatever he needed to do, but she wanted to spend time getting back to herself. She started going to the women's ministry meetings at her local church and building relationships there. Instead of picking up around the house like she did every evening after dinner, she gave their three kids chores to do and used her new free time to go out to get coffee with friends. She even started taking art classes, something she had always wanted to do.

After a few months of this, she could feel her rage toward Marcus lessening. She was still hurting, of course, but she didn't feel like her world was ending anymore. She knew that no matter what happened between her and her husband, she was still a child of God and she was loved.

Now it was time for their nightly game. Marcus would try to connect with his wife and Evelyn would either block it or accept, depending on how she was feeling that day.

"These are for you," she said, motioning toward a thick stack of envelopes. "The kids already ate and there's some leftover lasagna in the fridge if you want it." She stood up and yawned. "I'm tired. I think I'm going to go upstairs, take a shower and then go to bed."

Marcus glanced at the clock. "It's seven-thirty."

"I know what time it is," Evelyn said, making her way to the steps.

For months now, Marcus had been trying to give Evelyn space to feel what she was feeling and allow her to heal. But tonight, something felt different, so he followed her upstairs.

"What are you doing?" she asked, wrapping the towel around her body.

"I just wanted to talk to you," he said, sitting down on the side of the tub. "I feel like I haven't seen you all week. You've been out almost every night."

Evelyn picked up her shower cap and stretched it over her hair. "What do you want to talk about?"

Marcus fidgeted a bit. Starting conversations were always tricky these days but he felt her pulling away. "How are you doing this week?"

She shrugged. "I'm fine. Just been trying to figure out what *I* want."

"And what do you want?"

"Peace of mind. A place for me to just be me. Honesty. Romance."

He nodded. "And am I included in that list of things you want?"

Evelyn paused for a long moment and readjusted her towel. "Maybe."

This was the first time since he had made his confession that Marcus felt truly hopeful about their future. He couldn't help but smile.

"We've still got a long way to go," she cautioned. "But... I've let go of a lot of anger."

"I promise you," he said, "I messed up but I'm here. I'm committed. I love you. And as long as it takes for you to forgive me and move forward with our relationship, that's how long I'm willing to wait."

pICkInG Up tHe pIeCes

Imagine you're in the kitchen and you accidentally knock a glass off the counter. It falls to the floor and shatters. What do you do?

First you freeze and take a look at the damage. How far did the pieces travel? Are there any under the counters where they're not as visible?

Anyone who has ever been a little clumsy knows that it's those little pieces, the ones that are almost invisible to the naked eye, that can cause problems if you don't sweep them up right away.

Days will pass and you'll walk across that floor barefoot and — ouch!

In reconciling with each other, your job is to sweep up those little pieces. The surface stuff — the betrayal, dishonesty, lack of intimacy — is easy to fixate on, but it's not the true cause of the tension in your marriage. Scripture says, "Catch for us the foxes, the little foxes that ruin the vineyards, our vineyards that are in bloom" (Song of Solomon 2:15 NIV).

And now you're ready for this stage. Only after you've gone through the first two steps of reconciliation — first reconciling to God and then reconciling to yourself — can you move on to the final step: reconciliation with each other.

By this point in the process, you might be itching to get to work on your marriage. You've prayed, you've put in work on yourself, and now you're ready to mend one of your most important relationships.

Keep the following in mind as you work to restore the peace in your marriage.

forGIveness

In the last chapter, we talked about forgiveness and how crucial it is for both parties in a shattered marriage to forgive themselves for their role in whatever happened. Forgiveness is a powerful gift, and when we share it with ourselves, it allows us to release the pain of the past and give ourselves a fresh new start.

When you're in the midst of it, forgiving your *partner* can be a different thing all together. If you feel wronged, you may still be replaying the offense in your head and using all your mental energy to figure out what went wrong.

Shattered

Carrying that burden is exhausting! If for no other reason, forgiveness is a release from baggage, which is why we (and most other relationship experts) recommend it. Part of the reason it's so hard is that we're stuck in the past. We want to accept an apology. The other person may not ever admit they were wrong. Even if they never admit their role in the situation, you can still make a conscious decision to forgive them for their actions.

It won't be like it was. You're holding on to hope for a better past. You will never get that back. As opposed to spending all that time wishing it was a better past, how about working toward a better future. That means there's hope. That's what this book is about.

Here are four things to keep in mind:

1. Forgiveness doesn't happen overnight.

2. Forgiveness doesn't mean you'll automatically be "back to normal."

3. Forgiveness doesn't automatically erase all your negative feelings about the event.

4. Forgiveness can bring you peace, but only if you commit to it.

The process of forgiving someone is kind of like a line dance — two steps here, turn around, step to the right, and eventually you have something resembling peace of mind. But there will be ebbs and flows. You'll be tempted to re-hash old arguments. You might feel great, and all of a sudden something will trigger you and the pain will feel fresh.

But you have to keep pressing on, and forgiveness is the way forward.

Shattered

There are three essential steps to forgiveness:

1. Acknowledgment

2. Decision

3. Release

First, you must acknowledge whatever is holding you back. If your spouse was unfaithful or betrayed you in some other way, you must accept the pain of their actions and understand that they made a mistake. They are flawed and they took actions that weren't acceptable for you. It doesn't make it okay, but accepting your current reality is key.

Then you have to make a decision to forgive. Forgiveness is promising to honor yourself by not living in the past. No amount of praying and wishing will change what happened. The only way out is through. Remember: some situations don't have a solution. You will drive yourself crazy trying to investigate and hold your spouse accountable in your own public court. Let it go and let God bless you.

Then you can release the pain. It may not feel good in the moment, but you are now stronger because of this incident. It taught you more about yourself — most of all, how you handle pain and disappointment.

tHree-Cord StrenGtH

One of our favorite Bible verses, which we always include in our marriage presentations, is Ecclesiastes 4:9-12:

> *Two are better than one, because they have a good reward for their labour. For if they fall, the one will lift up his fellow. But woe to him that is alone when he*

falleth, for he hath not another to help him up. Again, if two lie down together, then they have heat, but how can one be warm alone? And if one prevail against him, two shall withstand him; and a three-strand cord is not quickly broken. (KJV)

God tells us that while two is good, three is greater. There should be three parties in your marriage: you, your spouse, and God. This is because as humans we are fallible and prone to mistakes. But if God is in the midst of your relationship, He can fill those holes and keep the two of you connected.

Contrary to popular belief, marriage is not 50-50. There are times we do not always have what we need as individuals and as a couple. In times of challenges, times when we cannot reach our spouse, or times when our needs are not being met by the other, it is God who makes up the difference. In fact, as we said prior, God should not be a second thought or a plan B, but should be our first point of contact. When things are in disarray, it is probably because we have to realign ourselves with God as individuals and as a couple.

We cannot tell you how often God has rescued us from us. There have been many situations in which we had reached an impasse, and God spoke to both of us, giving us grace and wisdom to resolve the situation and move forward. Having God as the third strand in our marriage keeps us bound in faith and in love.

When we aren't seeing eye to eye, I (Naomi) turn to God as our mediator. I'll remind myself that Joel is God's son. I love him, but God loves him first and therefore, if I can't reach him, I'll take him to the Lord in prayer.

I (Joel) trust God to help me step my husband game up. My favorite prayer is, "God, this is your baby girl, and right now I don't know how to give her what she needs. Will you please show me how to love my wife the way she needs to be loved?"

davId and paM

When Pam heard David's footsteps approaching the bedroom, she instinctively contemplated whether she should pretend to be asleep. That had been her go-to move over the past few months as they tried hard to dig themselves out of their financial hole. She was shocked to learn how bad things had gotten in such a short amount of time, but she wasted no time trying to get things in order.

After she saw the eviction notice and David's reluctance to reach out to his parents for help, she reached out to them herself. They had been happy to give them some money to stay afloat.

To her surprise, David had started driving for a ride-sharing company, which brought in a little money while he continued to look for a job. The extra money was nice and allowed them to keep their heads above water until they could truly feel like they were on their feet.

Finances aside, their marriage was still like walking on eggshells. David tried to be more transparent with the bills and Pam started joining him once a week to talk about their budget. She was still struggling to trust him, so she thought this was the best way to handle their issues. She was stunned because he had never been this irresponsible before. David had always been worried about her and their daughter, so discovering that he would quietly let them sink into eviction was pretty rattling.

Pam felt like she was back being a single mom, counting every penny, praying that she would have more money than bills each month. She had thought she was past that "robbing Peter to pay Paul" lifestyle and resented David for triggering those feelings of financial insecurity.

David, on the other hand, was quietly kicking himself. He couldn't believe their money problems had snowballed so quickly either. It seemed like bills had come out of nowhere. There was a car repair they hadn't anticipated, and they had to take their daughter to the ER one night, which left them with a $500 medical bill. Their savings had been sucked dry. But David hadn't wanted Pam to worry. On their wedding day, he had promised her that he would take care of her and she wouldn't have to stress about money like she did when she was a single mom. He could feel her disappointment all over her face and in her body language every time they were in the same room.

After Pam went to his parents for money to keep them from getting evicted, his dad stopped by. This was one of the reasons David hadn't wanted to reach out for help — he didn't want his parents to know he failed.

His father, Paul, came over and sat opposite his son in the living room. "You know your mother and I are here for you whenever you need us. We were happy to give you whatever money you needed. So please tell me what's going on."

David took a deep breath and gave his father the shortened version. His dad sat there and nodded thoughtfully.

"Well, I can see why Pam came to us," he said. "I'm glad she did."

"I'm glad she did too."

"But you know, son, you don't have to be ashamed," his dad told him. "It's what you do from here that really matters."

"What do you mean?"

"Well, have you apologized to your wife?"

"Of course."

"Did you really?"

"Kind of," David admitted. "I mean, I told her I was sorry. We haven't really talked much though."

"You've got to make amends," his dad told him. "You can't make her forgive you, but you can put your best foot forward to make sure she knows that you're trying your best." He paused for a minute. "Let me ask you a question."

"Yes?"

"Have you prayed for her?"

David was quiet. "Prayed for her?"

"Yes. Prayed for her." He leaned forward. "I have no doubt that you two will pull through this. But right now, you need some help. Prayer could be what turns this whole thing around."

CoMMIt to prayer

At times, reconciling with your partner can require more strength than you think you have. That's when you can call on God to help you pull through.

But God wants to hear from us regularly. He wants to hear our concerns, our questions, our testimony. We always say that God is a strong God — He can handle our stresses and frustrations better than we can. And the beautiful thing is, He loves us and wants us to flourish. So when you turn to God in prayer, He only wants the best for you. There's no second-guessing here. It's refreshing to have that type of relationship in your life, especially when you're fighting for your marriage.

Set aside time every day to go to God. Our favorite prayer is this: "God, please remove everything from me that's not of You."

Baptized SuBMIssIon to eaCH OtHer

Our pastor, the Rev. Dr. Alan Ragland, says, "The word and practice of submission need to be baptized." He teaches — as we also believe, live, and teach in our consultations — that submission is a mutual mandate of both partners committed to a higher purpose! God's purpose. Submission is not a dirty word. It is a word of honor and respect for both spouses. Rev. Dr. Ragland teaches that submission means we align ourselves under the mission of the other. Ephesians 5:22 is commonly used to teach women to submit to their husbands: "Wives, submit to your own husbands, as to the Lord" (ESV). However, we must back up to Ephesians 5:21, where the Bible clearly admonishes both the husband and the wife to submit to God and then to one another: "Submit to one another out of reverence for Christ" (NIV). We believe that men and women are equals. We do not teach that women are second-class citizens. We understand that the whole purpose of this text is to bring clarity to the roles of men and women in relationship, and also their needs. Paul points out that the basic needs of men are respect and honor, and the basic need of women is to feel cared for and secure in the relationship. If these two needs are not met, the marriage suffers. Therefore, submission is not about the propensity to cause oppression to the woman or to make her feel subservient, but instead, it is a place of trust and loving devotion for both the man and woman.

denIse and CHarles

"We're surprised to see you out," said Tamika, Denise's friend, as she sipped her margarita. "We hardly ever see you anymore."

"Yeah," her friend Kim chimed in. "You've been ducking us."

Denise shook her head. "Not even close."

It had been several months since Denise had gone home and told her husband Charles about her emotional affair with Marvin. Predictably, he had been angry and wanted to rush to Marvin's house to have it out with him. Denise managed to calm him down and remind him that while they had gotten close, they had never gotten physical with each other.

"Is that supposed to make me feel better?" Charles snapped. "I've got another man walking around here thinking he knows my wife better than I do. That's foul, Denise."

Denise winced. "I said I'm sorry."

"And this has been going on for *months*. I've shaken this guy's hand and you never told me anything about him. Y'all go to lunch together every week, huh?"

She just nodded.

"And who pays?"

"Um . . . he does."

"So he's buying you lunch every week. And what do you talk about?"

"Work. Family stuff."

Charles exhaled loudly. "Man."

"I just thought I should tell you—"

"You talk to him about me?"

"What?"

"Do you talk to him about me? When I get on your nerves do you run to him to complain?"

"Charles . . ."

"Just answer the question."

Denise paused but decided to be truthful. "Yes."

"Wow." Charles threw his arms up and started pacing. "Well… I don't know what you want me to say. You work with this guy, so I can't just say I don't want you to see him again."

"I promise things will be different," Denise said.

"How?"

She thought for a moment. "When I sat there at lunch today, I could see that we had gone too far and I wanted to stop everything before we did something we'd both regret. You and I may have our problems, but I do love you. I don't want to hurt you more than I already have."

Charles didn't respond, but kept pacing.

"Charles . . ."

"What?"

"I'm sorry."

"You keep saying that."

Shattered

They had gone around and around for the rest of the night. Denise was exhausted the next morning, when she had to go to work and navigate the tricky situation with Marvin. She told him that she would no longer be able to do their Monday lunches, and she needed to create appropriate boundaries. He was gracious and agreed to give her space as she worked to repair her marriage.

In the months since, Denise's relationship with Charles had been full of ups and downs. They'd had more than one screaming match while they tried to move forward, and Denise wasn't sure if they were going to make it.

Charles was furious. Though Denise and Marvin hadn't been physical, he knew his wife. He knew that having someone be there for her emotionally was even more intimate than sex.

But while he was angry at her, he couldn't help but be a little angry at himself too. How many times over the past year had he gone in the basement to watch basketball instead of sitting with his wife and asking about her day? How many times had she invited him to come to a work event with her and he said he was too tired? It was clear how Marvin had managed to hold such a strong place in her heart—Charles had left the door wide open.

As time had progressed, Denise noticed that Charles seemed less angry. She would text him from work about things she used to share with Marvin and he would respond with a funny text. She felt like they were reconnecting in a way that they never had before.

Now, they were on good enough terms that Denise felt like she could exhale. To celebrate not feeling like enemy number one in her house, she had decided to go out for drinks with her friends and rehash how things had been going over the past few months.

"So y'all are good now?" Kim asked.

"We're better," Denise said. "Every day is different, but I think we're over the worst of it."

"Men have such a hard time forgiving women," Tamika said, knowingly. "So it's good you two are working through it. Charles is a good guy."

Denise smiled. "That he is."

"So have you talked to Marvin?" Kim asked. "Is he still . . . around?"

"Not really," Denise said. "We were always with different clients, so there isn't much overlap in our work. Once I told him that we couldn't continue what we were doing, he fell back. Last I heard, he got engaged."

"Wow, really?" Kim said.

"Yeah," Denise said. "So he's good."

"You miss him?" Tamika asked.

"Not really," Denise said truthfully. "I realized that I was leaning on Marvin because I wasn't getting what I needed from Charles. Not that Charles was to blame. But I wasn't speaking up for myself. I wasn't putting forth that effort. And now that we're *both* working at it, it's like we have a whole new marriage."

"Well, I'll drink to that," Kim said, holding her glass high. The trio clinked their glasses together and ordered another round.

WorkInG on tHe BiG tHree

After your marriage is tested, then the real fun begins.

Fun? you might be thinking. *Nothing about this is fun!*

Think back to the best part of your relationship. Chances are, it was the beginning. Everything was fresh and new. You never ran out of things to talk about. Even doing regular, everyday things like going to the movies was fun because it was your first time doing it together.

Now that you are working to piece your relationship back together, you have to get to know each other all over again. You're going to date each other. You're going to build something new that's even better than what you had before.

The three pillars of a strong relationship — communication, trust, and intimacy — are all interconnected. In the beginning of the book, we talked about how over the course of a relationship these three pillars can be shaken and shattered. Now we'll discuss how to rebuild and make it better than ever.

Build CoMMunICatIon

While you're working to rebuild your relationship, you need to be intentional about the time you spend together. That may mean cutting back on hanging out with your friends or staying late after work. If you have kids, that might mean getting a babysitter and making it a point to get out of the house together at least weekly.

Do what you can to find activities that encourage conversation. Sitting in a dark theater for two hours and then driving home might not be the type of date night your marriage needs at the moment. Tap into your hobbies and interests to find activities that both of you might enjoy. Maybe you'll go skating together and share stories of how you used to go to the skating rink in high school. Maybe you'll go to a paint-and-sip night and tap into your artistic side together.

Whatever it is, clear the air for great conversation by minimizing distractions. That means putting away the cell phone, turning off the TV, and putting the kids to bed. Relationship author Jackie Bledsoe calls his quality time with his wife "parent meetings." They lock the door and spend an hour or so every day catching up with each other. Their children know this is "mommy and daddy time," so they don't try to interrupt.[1]

The key is to be consistent. Remember how much time you invested into your relationship in the beginning, back when it was effortless? That's what you need to do now. Don't think you already know everything about your spouse. Go into it like this is your first date. Try to put your best foot forward. Remember when you had a first date with someone and you made sure to clean out your car first? Go back to *that* level of interest.

Joel likes to remind women that communication is not just verbal but nonverbal as well. Often wives are looking for their man to sit and talk with them but sometimes their actions speak loudly and the wives miss it. If they bring home your favorite flavor of ice cream or caress your leg while sitting next to you, that's communication as well.

Build trust

The only way to rebuild trust is to be trustworthy. That part is pretty simple. Trust is something that can be rebuilt over time, and the onus is on the person who broke the trust to make sure the wounded party knows they can be trusted again.

The most important part of building trust is transparency. Secrets and lies flourish in the dark, so being open is always important, particularly during this period. Set some ground rules for what the wounded party needs to feel more comfortable. Perhaps that's to share passwords for a little while or to give regular assurances that they are committed and ready to fight for their marriage.

But while the person who messed up should lead the charge, the other party has to be certain to extend grace. This is where forgiveness comes in. It can be tempting to lash out and rehash your pain, but it only serves to keep the wound fresh. If you want to move forward, you have to *move forward*.

Build IntIMaCy

Again, intimacy is not just about sex, but about all the things leading up to *and* including sex. When a marriage is strained, sex is usually one of the first things that go out of the window. This is understandable, as sex is one of the most intimate things you can do with someone you love. But sex is also healing and can reconnect us again.

If you're not quite there yet, find other ways to bring physical touch into the relationship. Run a bath for the other person. Lay your head on their shoulder. Hold hands while you're out together. If you're not ready for sex, try to get back in the habit of kissing regularly. One couple we know makes it a point to kiss at least twice a day — once when they leave each other to go to work and once when they're back together at the end of the day.

Besides physical touch, you can also build intimacy by making what relationship expert John Gottman calls "bids." Each time you invite your partner into your world, that's a bid. A bid could be something as simple as asking your spouse to sit next to you while you watch TV or sharing a funny video you saw online. Accepting bids from your partner allows you two to connect and learn about each other, which strengthens intimacy.

Hard Work Pays Off

All of these action steps will take time. You won't necessarily see a change in your relationship overnight, but in time, you'll see your conversations get lighter, the tension lift and the laughter return.

You won't be as anxious in each other's presence and you'll begin to remember why you fell in love with each other in the first place.

We'd be remiss if we didn't say that in the best-case scenario, both parties are working on their relationship together. It's hard to heal a marriage by yourself. But even if the other person isn't as committed to healing the relationship, if you undergo this process and put forth 100% effort, you can say that you gave it your all. You won't have any regrets at the end of the day.

Chapter Five

Doing the Work

In each of the previous chapters, we've opened with fictional stories based on couples we've consulted over the years. These stories were a composite of common themes we see arise most often in our work, ones that we felt would resonate with most readers.

Now we want to get more personal with you and share some of the biggest hurdles we've had to encounter in our marriage. Our intention in writing this book was to be transparent. Often when reading pieces of marriage advice, the author tends to focus on what they know and have studied, not necessarily on what they've experienced. We want to share both, to let you know that we are not just telling you how to repair your marriage, but that these tools have helped repair our marriage as well.

In fact, as we were writing this book, we celebrated our fifteenth wedding anniversary, a day that at times in our marriage we weren't sure we would reach. On social media, we both posted our anniversary wishes to each other and the comments and likes came rolling in. By the end of the day, we had more than 200 likes on each of our posts.

We love feeling the support of our community, but we know that as spiritual leaders, there is a tendency to gloss over the real-life issues we might have and instead peg us as "relationship goals."

Even with Jesus as the center of our marriage, we have still had to work hard at our relationship. God wants us to grow through marriage, so that means that sometimes the path is bumpy. This has been a great ride, but it hasn't been without pain or sacrifice. We've had to learn to balance and find harmony. Harmony for us means that we won't be able to give everything equal time or equal energy at all times; however, we must be flexible and able to discern what deserves our time and energy in our marriage. We've had times when we have been in over our head. That's when the third cord—God—proved even more valuable. Without His strength, we don't know if we would have made it through.

So this is where we get to be vulnerable. We ask that you read this chapter with an eye toward understanding who we are as people. We've worked through many of our issues before presenting them here, and we're proud to be able to share lessons from our marriage to help so many others.

In all the previous sections of this book, we have used one voice to share our thoughts on the steps of reconciliation, but now we're going to go deeper and more personal. Here you'll hear from us separately, first Naomi then Joel, so you can see how even in the same marriage, two people often have different perspectives of the same situation. We challenge you to read and really listen, no matter whose "side" you might originally feel drawn to.

n_{aoMI} S_{ays}

I was thirty-eight when I married Joel. I had spent a long time thinking about what type of man I wanted to marry and I prayed to God regularly for such a man to come my way. Immediately, God led me to Proverbs 31 and challenged me to prepare myself to be the type of wife this husband *I wanted* would be looking for. I had a lot of work to do. I know I don't measure up to this woman, however, God is continuing to teach me how to be the wife my husband needs. He also continues to increase my capacity to manage all that He is blessing my life with. Each day is a learning opportunity.

I met Joel in church, where we were friends years before we began dating. Interestingly enough, as friends, we actually prayed for each other to have the mate they desired. Our love and wishes for each other were so pure. We truly wanted the best for each other, just from the level of friendship we had.

Joel was the first to realize that he had deeper feelings. When he first told me, I wasn't ready to take our relationship a step further, so we had to back off for a while until I felt ready to be with him on a romantic level.

But once we decided to make it official, it was an amazing relationship. Joel was a bit younger than I, but it didn't even seem to matter much. I felt loved and cherished as his girlfriend, so when he proposed, it felt like God was moving in both our lives.

As we mentioned in the introduction, we dedicated our marriage to God because we wanted to honor Him for bringing us together. We were strong in our commitment and it showed.

We quickly got pregnant after the wedding and welcomed our twin boys into our family. Two years later, we welcomed our daughter, and we were working hard to find our rhythm as a family of five.

When I talk to Joel now, we both agree that the first seven years of our marriage were blissful. We had our normal struggles, but everything was good. It took just about that long for us to get in the swing of things and get our footing. Joel was in seminary and working a full-time job. I was learning how to take care of two babies, then the third baby.

During this season, our marriage did not suffer, because we

tackled everything together. We turned toward one another. We faced issues as a team. It wasn't until after the fact that we realized we were having our own private storms.

We had enjoyed being intimate in our marriage, even after our twins were born, but after our third child, it slowed down significantly. My husband's love language is touch. He is the type of man who needs touch to feel connected — not just physically, but emotionally as well. I was busy tending to the children and going to seminary while he was working and carrying the load of being the breadwinner for the family. I don't think I was giving him what he needed emotionally. But he didn't pressure me in any way to give more of myself at a time where I felt like I had nothing left in the tank.

I soon felt like something wasn't quite right. Things felt like they were "off." You know how a woman's intuition (discernment) can tell her things? Mine was heightened.

Around this time, my husband went on a week-long business trip to the West Coast, leaving me and the kids at home in Chicago to miss him dearly. I know Joel was probably happy to get out of the house and have some time to himself for a change. I was happy for him as well and encouraged it, as he usually came straight home and spent most of his time with us. I didn't expect him to be readily available whenever I called, but I found it strange that on this trip, I was having a hard time getting in touch with him or when he did answer, our conversations were brief.

I realized that it was a five-city tour and the work he and his team were doing was rigorous, with long days and few breaks. However, I was beginning to get worried that maybe he was doing something he shouldn't be doing out there. One day during the trip, he was on the phone with me and ordered some room service to be sent up to his room. When it came, I overheard the hotel staff member tell him, "I hope you and your lady enjoy your meal."

Shattered

My warning bells immediately went off!

To his credit, Joel didn't get flustered like he was caught in a lie. He simply told the man that he was mistaken – there was no woman in the room. He had just ordered something to eat while he relaxed in his room. But if you think that did anything to calm me down, you'd be wrong.

By the time he got back, I was on fire. We went around and around – me hurling accusations at him, and him trying to defend himself, telling me he did nothing wrong. I was angry and hurt, and didn't feel like fighting for something I felt God had given us. I didn't know what to think. The room service comment on its own might not have raised suspicions if he hadn't also been so hard to get a hold of all week. Should I trust what he was telling me or hold on to the suspicions I felt in my gut?

Things between us got even more tense. I had to reflect on how we got to this point. How had something that started out so strong devolved into silent treatments and tears?

I had made up in my mind about all these things he was allegedly doing, because that's how much it hurt me that he didn't trust me enough to come to me with what he needed in the relationship, which was a safe place to share what he was feeling. When he took that trip, he felt freedom like he hadn't in a while, away from the daily pressures of being the breadwinner.

So while I looked at his behavior, I also had to take a step back and look at what I was doing – I automatically expected the worst from him.

I didn't have a relationship with my father growing up. The only relationships I had with men at that time were with my brothers and my uncles. I was raised by three strong women, and their example of relationships with men was very poor. I had no role models, no guidance on what a healthy relationship with a man was supposed to look like, outside of my pastor and my spiritual dad, in my latter years, who taught me how real men treated their wives. So I was very green. Joel wasn't supposed to betray me – he was supposed to love me like Jesus loved the church, *right?*

I realized I had romanticized what it would be like to have this husband after I waited. I don't think I was thinking about his humanity. I had this love affair going with God. When he sent me my husband, Joel couldn't measure up to this ideal I had in my head. It wasn't his fault. I had put him in this space where only God could be. Joel loves me, but he isn't perfect. Although I didn't expect him to be perfect, I did expect him to be faithful. This situation brought me back to reality.

As a Christian woman, I had some unrealistic expectations. When we first got married, it took me a minute to adjust. Every night as a single woman, I would spend time with the Lord. Then I would wake up and pray. The other side of my bed was reserved for my books, which I spent hours on end reading and studying. When Joel came in, it was like, "So where do I sleep?" I had not made room for him in my bed. The Lord revealed that I had not yet made room for him in my life either. I didn't accept his help.

But in correcting that, I went too far left. I made room for Joel and left little space for God. It was vitally important to find balance. I love Joel and I need him. I was this independent woman when he found me, but later ended up putting too much pressure on him to be there.

Our friendship has saved us so many times. If we had not been friends first, if our relationship hadn't been built on God, I think we could have been in trouble. Even through all the arguments and pain, I still loved him as my friend.

We still struggled for years to rebuild our trust. We ultimately did go to counseling. It's part of the reason we are now consultants to other couples. We absolutely see the value in it and the way it has transformed our marriage. Some of the tools we learned in therapy we still use today, especially as it relates to triggers and communication.

To get our marriage back on track, it was an "all of the above" effort—counseling, our friendship, our reliance on God. It was a daily commitment to stay above the fray.

We teach that we all have triggers, so we have to identify them. We have to acknowledge them. Don't rehearse them over and over again. Keep the memories as well as the scars. Press forward. There is still more—we have not arrived at our final destination. It's important to move forward, not to stay stagnant. Anything that's staying still can become stale. Trust that there's more to come that's worth fighting for.

The biggest lesson I've learned is that when we expect others to fill the void, we get into trouble. We tend to get needy and look to our spouse to fill us up when we're low. Now I know better. That void needs to be filled by God. When I know I'm depleted and I have too high expectations of my husband, it's because I haven't spent enough time with God.

It was easy for me to try to use my spouse or my children to fill those needs. We were going to church every Sunday, but I hadn't been having my personal time with God. As a result, I became thirsty and was expecting other people to quench my thirst. But that failed. That's when I started trying to restore my relationship with God. It was then that I turned back to God.

Reconciliation is incumbent upon forgiveness, but you don't always get an apology. We don't wait for an apology. It's a gift we choose to give the other person. It's not for them; it's for us. If we choose not to forgive, we'll continue to rehash the pain and let it eat away at us. It's a conscious decision to say, "I forgive you." Even if the other person is at fault, we cannot allow it to hold us hostage. Forgiveness doesn't say we're weak or that we allow people to walk over us. Being vulnerable in a relationship, is risky on both sides. We have to sit with these questions: "What role did I play in this? What role *will* I play in this?" I am not saying that we have to take on the fault of the other person, or minimize the impact of the betrayal or infraction, but we cannot allow it to eat away at our hearts and cause us to die inside or kill our spouse in the meantime. Sometimes we rehash things to the point where our spouse can't even get up from under the weight of the accusations. In marriage, we can choose to move forward and love our spouse again. The journey forward may not be easy, but it will be worth it.

After much prayer, doubt, many tears, unforgiveness, and bitterness, I decided not to let my dream marriage end in a nightmare. Thank God for being the cord that bound our hearts, even when we were ready to let go.

Joel Says

My parents have been married for fifty-one years. I sit and look at my wife and I hope that we too can get to fifty years of marriage one day. However, I know that there are many couples who are celebrating their golden anniversaries and are completely and utterly unhappy. There's a difference between surviving and thriving.

As I sit to write this, I am so thankful to have Naomi as my wife. We've had fifteen years of marriage together and while they haven't all been smooth, they've all been worth the investment.

I was the one who fell for her first, at the very beginning of our relationship. I fell in love with her spirit and the way she cared for those around her. She was an incredible listener, a great friend, and a beautiful woman. As Proverbs 18:22 says, "He who finds a wife finds a good thing, And obtains favor from the Lord" (NKJV) I knew in Naomi I had found favor.

I'll admit that I am not now nor have I ever been a perfect husband and father. Lord knows I have made my share of mistakes trying to figure out how to be all that my wife and children need from me.

But my biggest mistake was not letting my wife in on that journey. We had to learn how to grow together. I married a strong black woman and I know what that means now. Even though I knew Naomi loved me and was happy to have me, she still operated independently. She hadn't accepted the fact that she had a partner in this thing called life. For example, in the early months when we had the twins, whenever we would be going somewhere, we'd have to pack at least two of everything — like Noah. Naomi would try to carry everything. She had the babies, the diaper bags — and my hands were empty. I'd go to assist her and she'd say, "I have it." I had to realize that she came from an environment where women took care of themselves and each other because they had to. It took a while for her to accept that while she didn't need me, it was a blessing to have my help.

For the first seven years of our marriage, we only had small struggles like that. We were so busy just trying to catch up with the new demands of our life that we didn't even have a minute to catch our breath. We still enjoyed one another in every way. We were creative in finding time for intimacy around our schedules and around our children.

It wasn't until around the eighth year of our marriage that we began to notice the cracks in the windshield.

It was a heavy period. We were fortunate that we were able to support our whole family on my one salary while Naomi stayed home with the kids, but things weren't going as smoothly as we hoped. I honestly began feeling neglected, as I was carrying this weight as the breadwinner. But I wasn't being honest in sharing how I felt. I just kept saying, "It's okay and we can make it."

I felt like I had to be Superman out in the world, but then when I got home, I wasn't allowed to be Clark Kent. I had to be Superman at home too. I felt like I would be less of a man if I didn't have it all together. I was raised in a family where my father would work and just come put his check on the table. That shaped my feelings about money and finances too. I wasn't proactive about our household budget and wasn't comfortable budgeting, which contributed to the stress.

A lot of my struggles with fatherhood came from my upbringing. When I was a child, my father was a truck driver and would be gone four or five nights out of the week. He was a hard worker and did the best he could to keep a roof over our heads. But we also didn't get much time with him, because when he had time off on the weekends, he used that opportunity to hang out with his friends or get some alone time. He wanted to release that steam from putting in so many hours on the road.

I decided that I didn't want to live that kind of distant life. I wanted to be there for my wife and children. I wanted them to see me every night. Looking back on it now, I realize I didn't have any balance either. That probably jarred things too. I was trying to be a committed husband first and spend extra time and attention on my wife to strengthen our new marriage. When we got together, we hardly ever went out with anyone else.

The first few years of our marriage were a huge adjustment — I went from being single to having a wife to having three mouths to feed. And once those kids came along, that became my whole focus. I had these people that I was responsible for, that I had to take care of. I wanted my wife to understand that if I was not as lovey-dovey as before, it was because I was out there pounding the pavement. I wanted to be an ultimate provider. You need it? I got it. No worries at all.

I looked up one day and asked, "How did we get here?" We were so busy and we weren't tuned into each other's needs. I realized that was partly because I wasn't letting Naomi know what my needs were!

When my work trip came up, I was looking at it as an opportunity for me to have a little fun and relax. I would only be responsible for myself for almost a week, and although I knew Naomi would have her hands full while I was gone, I was confident that she would have everything under control.

Now, I admit I messed up by not answering her calls like I should have. It raised suspicions and caused her to worry when truthfully nothing was going on. But I didn't help my case by trying to test out my new freedom while my wife was doing heavy lifting at home.

So when she was on the phone with me and the hotel staffer mistakenly wished me and my guest a good evening (when there was no one else in the room with me) her intuition was buzzing. I can't even say I blamed her!

But I wasn't looking forward to going home and dealing with the fallout. I knew I had to try to make this right and show her that even though we were going through a rough patch, I was still committed to her. She could trust me.

In our consulting practice, we've encountered many men and women who have broken trust in their relationship, and the one thing most of them have in common is that they want things to be fixed quickly. They're trying to do the right thing, but their spouses are slow to warm up to their efforts. They're like, "Can I at least get some credit? I'm actually trying. How long do I have to do this?" The pain is so great that they want to rush the process. But the pain didn't just start right away. It's in all the little things that added up before someone was finally pushed over the edge.

I have resolved in myself that in my marriage, I don't care how long it takes. I'm in it. It's hard not to want to defend yourself, but once I understand that it's part of the process, I'm willing to put that aside. If Naomi is my queen, then what won't I do to make her feel like my queen? If she's telling me what she needs, then why wouldn't I give it to her? The Lord let me know that if you want to be all-in, then be all-in.

In Psalm 51, after David committed adultery with Bathsheba, he told the Lord, "Against You . . . I have sinned" (Psalm 51:4 NKJV). That became one of the lenses through how I viewed this relationship. I made this vow to God. If I sin against Naomi, I'm not just sinning against her, but the Lord too.

I wanted to be a great husband, not only for myself, but for Naomi as well. She had really done the work individually. She had positioned herself for a great marriage, practicing abstinence for several years until we were wed. She had tried to do everything to please God. When we went through our challenges, it was even more compounded because she was feeling supreme disappointment. Why was our marriage not measuring up?

To move past this, we had to recommit ourselves to this marriage. Rebuilding trust is one day at a time, every day, making a decision to get back in the fight and open yourself up to trust again, to be vulnerable again. That's why the Lord shared it with us. We started by getting back to God, who is our source and resource. Getting back into that relationship with God enabled us to understand who we are as individuals. Self-esteem comes from God, not your mate or even yourself.

Shattered

That year, we started doing check-ins to be open and honest, and to give each other grace and forgiveness. We're still a work in progress. It takes consistency to deal with triggers and talk through them when they come up. We're in a better place in terms of being able to isolate the trigger. We're connected — I can feel a shift in her attitude. We promised that when things come up, we'll have the discussion.

I'm doing everything in my power to be more transparent with my wife. I've promised to keep communicating even when my instinct is to keep my feelings to myself. We have a regular date night, which allows us to simply be Naomi and Joel, without worrying about anything or anyone else. I had to learn to be more considerate. Now if I go on a trip, I wouldn't dare go days without checking in. (I shouldn't have done it the first time, but now I definitely know better.)

Together, we've worked to connect, even though we're busier than ever. We have returned to the beginning of our marriage, where we turned toward one another rather than away. The only time we turn our backs on each other, is to fight the enemy who often comes to steal, kill and destroy what we have built in God.

When people say marriage is hard work, it's all of this stuff. I hear a lot of "I shouldn't have to…" from guys — whether it's picking up flowers for your wife even though you think it's a waste of money, or taking her out even on those nights that the game is on. All of those things still matter and they're still important. And when trust is broken and the relationship is shattered, you have to go into overdrive if you want it to work.

Having hope in the face of what looks like an uphill battle is key. It reminds me of one of my favorite Scriptures, Jeremiah 18:1-6:

> *The word that came to Jeremiah from the Lord: "Come, go down to the potter's house, and there I will let you*

hear my words." So I went down to the potter's house, and there he was working at his wheel. The vessel he was making of clay was spoiled in the potter's hand, and he reworked it into another vessel, as seemed good to him. Then the word of the Lord came to me: Can I not do with you, O house of Israel, just as this potter has done? says the Lord. Just like the clay in the potter's hand, so are you in my hand, O house of Israel." (ESV)

This particular text talks about God making all things new. Even though we are marred, we are still in God's hands, and He has the power to turn things around with the ease of a skilled potter.

lessons learned

Even though we were living in the same household, with the same day-to-day life, we were both experiencing things very differently. We weren't communicating as well as we could have been and it led to a situation that could have been avoided if we had both been more honest about how we were feeling.

We've learned a lot over this fifteen-year marriage, but perhaps the biggest lesson of all is that we have to talk, talk, talk! It's not enough to have those surface-level conversations about housework or schedules. We have to insist upon being open with our innermost feelings -where we feel inadequate, what we are lacking in the relationship, and how open we are to change.

Being in love requires incredible vulnerability — you can't have a thriving marriage without it. The human urge is to protect yourself, but ultimately, it will cause more harm than good.

The second half of our marriage showed us that we had major work to do. We began our relationship with the best of intentions, but we shied away from doing real work that could have prevented our major blowup. This is what we mean when we say that there is no such thing as a perfect marriage. Even when you think things are going pretty well, once the storm comes, you will look back and see you missed a ton of warning signs.

This is not to say that all marriages are troubled — not in the slightest. But it does mean that you have to be vigilant and commit to daily action to strengthen your marriage. Think of your marriage in terms of your job. If your boss can never find you when they need you and your co-workers say you're always slacking off on big projects, you won't have that job for long. Same goes with a marriage. If you're not committed to the big goal and willing to put in the time and effort to sustain a marriage, then what are you doing?

are you ready?

Have you ever had a home repair that was way beyond your scope of expertise? You had to call an electrician or a plumber to come help solve the problem. When they showed up, they likely had a tool belt or a toolbox full of tools to help them solve the issue. While they might not have needed every tool they brought, it was good to be prepared with everything until they could pinpoint the problem and make note of what specific tools would be necessary.

We hope that in the same vein, we have equipped you with tools to help you make repairs in your marriage. We have packed a lot of advice and Scripture in these pages with the hopes that at least a handful of the knowledge would apply to your marriage and be the turning point to a better relationship.

For every reader who picked up this book, we hope that you understand a few key points:

1. We have to go back to the source — God — before we can heal from our hurt.

2. Understanding ourselves — what we need, how we can set boundaries, and how we love — has to happen first before we can repair a relationship with another.

3. Forgiveness is paramount. We cannot get to better days if we are still stuck in the past.

Continue on this journey with us. We want to help you go from good to even better, from good to greater. If you haven't already, stop by our website, TheMarriageInvestors.com, where we guide you through making these day-to-day choices that can help you rebound in your marriage and get back to happy. It *is* possible. You just have to take it one day at a time, one decision at a time.

In this last chapter, we wanted to leave you with a reminder that your relationship is what you make it. No relationship is perfect, so thinking the grass is greener (and easier) somewhere else isn't necessarily true.

Everything boils down to this: Are you ready and willing to fight for this relationship? Is there space for grace or an opportunity for growth?

These are questions only you can answer, but we hope that everything we've presented to you so far can help you make that decision.

As we stated in the Introduction, we hope this book has given you hope. When you're in the midst of a storm, it can be hard to feel that it will ever end. The forecast looks cloudy and gloomy as far as the eye can see. But we know the brighter days are on the horizon. We've seen it in our own marriage and in many others.

You just have to keep pressing forward and know that God can make all things new — including your marriage.

Shattered

Notes

Chapter 1

1. Gottman, J. M., & Silver, N. (2012). *What makes love last?: How to build trust and avoid betrayal.* New York, N.Y.: Simon & Schuster.

Chapter 3

1. Thomas, G. (2015). *Sacred marriage: what if God designed marriage to make us holy more than to make us happy?* Grand Rapids, MI: Zondervan.

2. Cloud, H., Townsend, J. S., & Guest, L. (2002). *Boundaries in marriage.* Grand Rapids, MI: Zondervan.

3. Gaspard, T. (2016, December 29). How Forgiveness Can Transform Your Marriage. Retrieved from https://www.gottman.com/blog/forgiveness-can-transform-marriage/

4. Can You Forgive. (n.d.). Retrieved from http://www.pbs.org/kqed/onenight/stories/forgive/

Chapter 4

1. Bledsoe, J. (2016). *The 7 rings of marriage: your model for a lasting and fulfilling marriage.* Nashville, TN: B & H Publishing Group.

Shattered

The Ministry of . . .

"Joel and Naomi offered us such useful insights into our current relationship and our future marriage during our pre-marital counseling sessions. The male-female perspective on marriage and relationships helped encourage us to deepen our compassion for each other. The 4 of us held hands in prayer for our session, our wedding, and our marriage at the beginning and ending of each session. Powerful!"

~ Tyehimba & Kelly Marie

•

"Vicki and I met at church several years ago and started a friendship that grew into something more … marriage! We were very different yet unique individuals because of vast backgrounds, and we were embarking upon a "blended" household! It was a blessing to receive pre-marital counseling that explored our unique personalities and common love of God and family. Our discussions and meetings with Rev. Joel and Rev. Naomi allowed us to understand this God-centered commitment that would change our lives forever!"

~ Will & Vicki

In their monumental work, Shattered, noted marriage and family consultants Joel and Naomi Mitchell have crafted a guide to the reconciliation of broken marriages. Using episodes from the lives of three couples to illustrate marriages in trouble, the authors establish their bona fides based on extensive counseling experience as well as moments from their own lives as a married couple. Marriages in trouble present different symptoms, but the core issue is one of reconciliation: with God, with oneself, and with one's partner. Shattered can be used as a stand-alone book or in combination with counseling or group study. The Mitchells do not disappoint!

~ Dr. Joyce Gay - Saint John Church-Baptist

•

Shattered: How to Overcome a Broken Marriage teaches couples how to create a brand new relationship from the pieces of a broken one. This book provides a biblically sound blueprint for husbands and wives to move from hurt to healed using God's word as the foundation and the Mitchells' sage wisdom for insight and inspiration. Read it now!

~ Lamar & Ronnie Tyler
Black and Married with Kids

•

It's evident that authors Joel and Naomi are anointed, gifted and passionate about bring healing to Shattered marriages and families. When reading Shattered, Luke 12:48 entered into our spirit "For unto whomsoever much is given, of him shall be much required." Shattered is the required tool for maintaining strong biblical and Christian marriages. Beware Shattered will arrest your comfortability, it is relevant to real life, easy to read, and you will be blessed by the transparency of Joel and Naomi! This is required Shattered proof arsenal for every marriage. God have given much to Ministers Joel and Naomi Mitchell and Shattered is undoubtedly the required.

~ David and Kelly Moses

•

Joel and Naomi Mitchell's Shattered: How to Overcome Brokenness In Marriage provides a dynamic assessment of the challenges that stunt the development of all marriages, it also displays that through individual spiritual growth and tactful communication, a marriage on the brink of failure can be restored. I assumed the issues that occupied my marriage only applied to my marriage. The Mitchell's analysis of conquering the ailments of marriage proves that through vigorous effort most relationships will be rescued. Married and soon to be married couples alike should read the Mitchell's powerful book in order to retrieve the resources to preserve our relationships.

~ Ed and Isela Morris

•

Do you want some practical and theological wisdom and encouragement on how to deal with the root of problems in marriage, rather than the symptoms of the problems in marriage? Do you want complete healing in marriage, rather than a temporary fix? This book is for you! Joel and Naomi Mitchell has put together a transformative tool that will change fractured marriages back into fruitful marriages. Shattered is a book that will give a healthy mixture of theology and transparency. The principles and exercises from this book has blessed my marriage in a tremendous way. I encourage you to study it and share it with other couples to bring fire back into their marriages.

~ Rev. Tyrone and Quincella Roberson

~ Invite ~

Joel & Naomi

The Marriage Investors partner with a diverse pool of faith-based communities, businesses, and individuals. Like us, they realize the importance of sharing resources, and investing in the wellness of marriages. Together, we are making the world stronger – by making individuals and families stronger.

We offer a variety of workshops and retreats for churches, businesses, and organizations. From romantic getaways to relationship forums, we also offer customized workshops and retreats.

We invite you to pick up a copy of the How to Shatter Proof Your Marriage Bundle which contains the book Shattered, The How to Shatter-Proof Your Marriage Workbook and the How to Shatter – Proof your Marriage Online Course by clicking the following link:

http://bit.ly/shatterproof-bundle

If you have any questions about the health of your marriage take the Shattered Quiz at www.TheMarriageInvestors.com

Joel and Naomi Mitchell
contact@TheMarriageInvestors.com

About the Authors
Joel & Naomi Mitchell

JOEL AND NAOMI MITCHELL are the founders of The Family and Marriage Institute of Chicago", a not-for profit organization that provides pastoral care and consulting to individuals and families, and The Marriage Investors, LLC, where they provide marriage consulting and coaching services. Together, they have extensive experience in ministry, social services, and consulting. They are ministers who love God and consider God an integral part of their marriage and their lives.

JOEL is an ordained and licensed minister who has worked in the field of social services for over 20 years. He is currently a Deputy Commissioner with the City of Chicago, and he oversees the day-to-day operations of the Human Services Division. Joel earned a Bachelor of Arts in Public Communication and Human Relations from Western Illinois University, and a Master of Divinity and Master of Theological Studies from McCormick Theological Seminary. He is presently pursuing his Doctor of Ministry in Pastoral Care and Counseling at Chicago Theological Seminary.

NAOMI is a licensed minister with a heart for wholeness, wellness, and well-being. In addition to a broad range of counseling expertise, she has extensive experience in the areas of bereavement, marriage, eating disorders, self-esteem, social adjustment, job loss, depression, and anxiety. Naomi earned a Bachelor of Science in Food and Nutrition from Southern Illinois

University, as well as a Master of Divinity and Master of Arts in Pastoral Care and Counseling from Garrett Evangelical Theological Seminary. She is currently a 2019 candidate for the Doctor of Ministry from the Association of Chicago Theological Schools, and is also a graduate of the Center for Religion and Psychotherapy, and is preparing to sit for the Licensed Clinical Professional Counselor's exam. Naomi is a Certified Prepare and Enrich Marriage Counselor and an approved Gottman Institute Couple's Check-up Advisor.

JOEL AND NAOMI have been married for fifteen years, and as a result, they have developed a heart and passion for working with married couples and families. Their mission is to restore wholeness by healing brokenness. They are committed to reconciling relationships, deepening love, and strengthening families. They believe that with the right tools and support, marriages can be restored, brokenness can be mended, and individuals can live a life filled with purpose, passion, and promise. They are the proud parents of three children, a set of 14-year-old twin boys, Jasper Caleb and Jacobi Israel, and an 12-year-old daughter, Sidni Joi.

Made in the USA
Monee, IL
13 April 2021